Euripides

Medea

Euripides

Medea

Translated by Diane Arnson Svarlien

Introduction and Notes by Robin Mitchell-Boyask

Hackett Publishing Company, Inc.
Indianapolis/Cambridge

For further information, please address

Hackett Publishing Company, Inc.
P.O. Box 44937
Indianapolis, Indiana 46244-0937

www.hackettpublishing.com

For information regarding performance rights,
please email us at Permissions@hackettpublishing.com

Cover design by Brian Rak and Abigail Coyle
Interior design by Meera Dash
Maps by William Nelson
Composition by William Hartman

Library of Congress Cataloging-in-Publication Data
Euripides.
      [Medea. English]
      Medea / Euripides ; translated by Diane Arnson Svarlien;
introduction and notes by Robin Mitchell-Boyask.
         p. cm.
      Includes bibliographical references.
      ISBN 978-0-87220-923-7 (pbk.)
      ISBN 978-0-87220-924-4 (cloth)
      1. Medea (Greek mythology)—Drama. I. Arnson Svarlien, Diane,
1960– II. Mitchell-Boyask, Robin, 1961– III. Title.

PA3975.M4S89 2008
882'.01—dc22

                                                    2007038719

Contents

Introduction[1]

Born sometime around 480 BCE, the Athenian playwright Euripides first entered the dramatic contest at the City Dionysia (also known as the Festival of Dionysus) in 455. His debut program included *The Daughters of Pelias,* a drama that depicted the murder of King Pelias by his daughters at the urging of the duplicitous barbarian princess Medea, then still desperate to assist her new husband, Jason. This play showed the new dramatist already exploring such issues as gender, marriage, ethnicity, and intrafamilial violence while demonstrating an almost lurid fascination with the more unseemly aspects of Greek myth. These themes would resurface throughout Euripides' career, perhaps most fully in the *Bacchae,* an extant drama he left unproduced at his death in 406, but not least in his *Medea.*

Though *Medea* is among the earliest of the surviving works of Euripides, it was first produced in 431 and is thus the product of a mature artist. It was, moreover, created at a crucial moment in Athenian history by a keen observer of that moment, an artist who passed from his early forties into his fifties as his home city of Athens moved from an almost unquestioned dominance of the political and cultural life of the Greek world to the early years of the Peloponnesian War against its rival city-state, Sparta.

Euripides and Athens in the Fifth Century

Euripides' life coincided with the span of almost the entire fifth century BCE, an era of breathtaking change in nearly every aspect of Greek life. That his dramas interact with these transformations and with the sheer level of agitation in Athenian society during that century's later decades probably accounts for much of the fascination with Euripides in our era, which has seen a comparable level of upheaval. The seeming modernity of Euripides, however, has fed into some stereotypes fostered by Euripides'

---

1. This Introduction is based on the author's Introduction to Euripides: *Alcestis, Medea, Hippolytus* (Indianapolis: Hackett Publishing, 2007).

contemporary, the comic poet Aristophanes, who mercilessly lampooned Euripides in a number of plays: by name in *Clouds,* and by making him a character in *Acharnians, Women at the Thesmophoria,* and, last but not least, *Frogs.* Aristophanes constantly mocked Euripides as the decadent purveyor of all cultural trends, a follower of the Sophists, an atheist, and an excessively bookish poet who staged fallen women and ruined heroes in rags. These comic dramas are largely responsible for Euripides' notoriety in subsequent centuries, and they certainly present caricatures, but since they also tap into the dynamic energy that circulated between Euripidean drama and the city of Athens in the fifth century, Aristophanes' portrayal of Euripides is a good starting point for this subject.

From his earliest surviving comedies to the first written after the death of Euripides, Aristophanes stressed the modern, revolutionary, and democratic aspects of Euripides and his dramas. He ridiculed both Euripides' artistic style and the content of his plots. In the first surviving comic drama, *Acharnians,* Aristophanes' hero Dicaeopolis needs to adopt a sympathetic—actually, pathetic—persona in order to defend himself against the hostile Acharnians, who are furious with him because of his personal truce with the Spartans. It occurs to him that Euripides must have an abundant supply of ragged beggar costumes, and so he visits the playwright while the latter is hard at work in his library (an unusual possession at that time, and perhaps one of the few details of Euripidean legend that was true). Euripides provides Dicaeopolis with the costume of Telephus, whose story of an outcast, wounded hero formed the basis of one of Euripides' plays in 438, thirteen years before *Acharnians.* Dicaeopolis then adopts not just the clothes but also the situation of Telephus in a scene parodying Euripides' tragedy, whose hilarity is especially remarkable because the tragic model is lost to us.

Two years later, in Aristophanes' *Clouds,* Strepsiades falls into a violent dispute with his son Pheidippides because junior refuses to sing a song from a drama by that paragon of virtue, Aeschylus. The father asks, "Why don't you come up with some of that clever modern stuff, something from one of those fashionable poets you're always going on about?" In response, Pheidippides "blurt[s] out some disgusting lines from Euripides, about a brother and sister going at it together!" Strepsiades reacts with dismay, and so his son in turn beats his father because he "dared to insult a gifted man like Euripides."[2] Euripides is thus represented as the flash point for the burgeoning generation gap in Athens during the 420s. Euripides returns as a character a dozen years later in *Women at the Thesmophoria* of 411. The Thesmophoria was an Athenian festival in honor of the goddess Demeter, during which women removed themselves from men for a period of three days and camped out, possibly in (of all places) the Pnyx, the meeting place of the Athenian Assembly. In Aristophanes' comedy, the women of Athens take advantage of their conclave to plot violence against Euripides because he has slandered them repeatedly in his plays. On the surface, this seems grossly unfair, for while Euripides does represent, for example, one woman as murderous in *Medea* and another in the throes of adulterous, quasi-incestuous, passion in his *Hippolytus,* he still depicts their motivations and situations with insightful sympathy. Moreover, there are very few women in Greek theater as unambiguously noble as the title character of his *Alcestis,* who sacrifices her own life for the sake of her husband. Yet Euripides' choice to recast heroic legend in terms of gender conflicts and domestic intrigue opened the door to the kinds of parodic simplifications that generate comedy in any era. As Euripides attempts to escape injury or even death at the hands of these angry women, Aristophanes engages in a wild burlesque of two of Euripides' plays: his now lost *Andromeda* and his *Helen,* which fortunately does survive.

The most telling portrayal of Euripides in Aristophanes comes six years later in *Frogs,* at a time when Athens was in the last desperate months of its long struggle with Sparta, and the city's sense of impending doom was heightened by the deaths of its most prominent tragic poets: Sophocles a few months earlier, and Euripides during the previous year, most likely during his self-imposed exile in the court of the king of Macedonia. Sophocles, an ancient source records, dressed himself in black for the Proagon, a preliminary ceremony at the City Dionysia, and brought his chorus in without garlands after news of his colleague's death had reached him. In Aristophanes' comedy, the god Dionysus mourns the death of Euripides and recognizes that none of the remaining poets are up to the job of entertaining and educating the citizens of Athens, and so he descends to the Underworld to retrieve Euripides. Yet,

---

2. Aristophanes, *Clouds,* translated by Peter Meineck (Indianapolis: Hackett Publishing, 2000), lines 1368–77.

upon his arrival, Aeschylus (who had died half a century before) and Euripides are fighting over the title of greatest playwright among the dead, and Dionysus is drawn into the struggle to such an extent that he presides over a contest between the two, with the winner allowed to return to the living with him. Aeschylus again is cast as the defender of the good old days and their good old ways, and Euripides as the decadent modernist. Nevertheless, Aeschylus himself is depicted as a pompous, often incomprehensible windbag, and the portrayal of a Euripides who "democratizes" high tragedy by allowing more realistic and lower-class characters is fair and generally on the mark. The competition affords opportunities for much silliness, yet a more sober thought recurs throughout, namely, that tragic poets have something to teach their city, that they make citizens better in some way. In the end, Euripides trips over his own sophistic witticisms and Dionysus chooses Aeschylus, who exits giving the strict command that Sophocles, not Euripides, should take his throne in the Underworld. Poor Euripides is thus defeated among both the living and the dead.

The form of Dionysus' response to Euripides' protest at his abandonment is a perfect example of the problems Aristophanes saw in Euripidean drama. Let us look at the passage (1469–75, my translation):

> EUR.: Remember now the oaths you swore to the gods
> that you'd take me back home. Choose your friends!
>
> DIO.: "My tongue is bound by oath . . ." I shall choose Aeschylus.
>
> EUR.: What have you done, most foul of men?
>
> DIO.: Me? I decided that Aeschylus wins. Why not?
>
> EUR.: You can look me in the face when you've done a most
> shameful deed?
>
> DIO.: "But what is shameful, unless it seems so to those who
> watch?"

Dionysus here throws two notorious Euripidean quotations back at their author (and even piles on a third in a response that follows the passage quoted above). Throughout all of these comic dramas, Aristophanes harps on the sophistic witticisms and the self-consciously rhetorical style of the speakers in the dramas of Euripides, who was so clearly and deeply affected by the flowering of the teaching of rhetoric in Athens by the Sophists during his lifetime in a way that

Sophocles, older by a decade, was not; while Sophoclean characters certainly often reflect the more formalized style of speech that was gaining popularity, they never sound so much like lawyers or (bad) politicians as Jason does in defending himself against Medea. The last line in the passage quoted above is an adaptation of Euripides' lost *Aeolus* and its original version, which ended "to those who do," is said to have shocked the Athenians, as did possibly the line from *Hippolytus,* "My tongue is bound by oath, but not my mind" (612, 673 Arnson Svarlien).[3] Sophistry, Aristophanes seems to suggest here, ultimately defeats itself. And while the *Hippolytus* quotation, taken out of context, is unfair to Euripides, since Hippolytus is destroyed because he *does not* violate his oath, it is easy to imagine such memorable lines being bandied about the streets of Athens and at evening drinking parties (*symposia*) where reciting poetry was one of the main activities.

Yet Aristophanes surely realized that Euripides was more the mirror reflecting the changes in society than the lamp lighting their way. Euripides' willingness to represent these changes and to depict heroes with the same problems, challenges, and speech as normal people, in a volatile mixture of myth and social realism—*that,* for Aristophanes, was the real issue. Aristotle, it is useful to recall here, preserves in *Poetics* 1460b35 Sophocles' observation that he himself "portrayed people the way they ought to be and Euripides the way they are." Thus, in *Medea,* we see the typical, mundane feminine concerns of the title character. Moreover, the conflicts in this play, as in other plays of Euripides, are cast in the rhetorical language and tactics taught by the Sophists, which had quickly taken over the courts and the Athenian Assembly and which had also been brought to bear on traditional morality; Jason's argument that in taking a new wife he acted "wisely and with restraint" and with love for Medea and her children is a prime example of such sophistry. Euripides thus was simply too big and easy a target. And as social controversy is always the comedian's bread and butter, Aristophanes needed Euripidean innovation and extremity. It could be that some of the wilder flights of fancy in Aristophanes were inspired by Euripides' pushing the limits of what was possible in

---

3. In this volume, all line references to the plays *Hippolytus* and *Alcestis* are from Arnson Svarlien's translations in Euripides, *Alcestis, Medea, Hippolytus* and are cited with the line range of the original Greek and then of Arnson Svarlien's translation, hereafter abbreviated AS.

the tragic theater by increasingly incorporating comic elements into
it. Aristophanes' relative neglect of Sophocles in *Frogs* suggests
that it was difficult to make much comic fodder out of a person
who was so universally admired and a poet who expressed a more
traditional view of the norms of Greek society. Euripides, tired of
losing to Sophocles and fed up with the ridicule from Aristophanes,
departed for Macedonia at some point late in his life, perhaps after
the production of his *Orestes* in 408; a failure in Athens, he was
now to become a poet in the court of the king of Macedonia.

At least that is what some of the biographical stories would have
us believe. Was Euripides really so unpopular in Athens? No. Much
evidence suggests the opposite. In recent years, scholars have shown
that many aspects of the received biographies of the ancient poets
are false (see Lefkowitz 1981), and the image of the embittered
poet, uttering views ahead of his time, exiled and then popular after
his death has proven too appealing to resist. Indeed, Scullion
(2003), who argues that the xenophobic comedy of Aristophanes
would surely have seized upon any sojourn in Macedonia and run
with it in *Frogs,* has recently questioned whether Euripides ever
made the trip at all. And Aristophanes would not have continually
picked on an individual who was not fundamentally prominent and
popular. Further, Euripides seems to have had an enormous impact
on Sophocles himself, as seen in the ruined heroes of his last two
surviving dramas, *Philoctetes* and *Oedipus at Colonus.* Several
decades after his death, Euripides was acclaimed by Aristotle,
despite the philosopher's preference for Sophocles, as "the most
tragic" of the poets. Moreover, two anecdotes from Plutarch in fact
show that Euripides was more popular than a mere victory list
would indicate. In the aftermath of Athens' disastrous expedition
against Sicily (415–413 BCE), a group of surviving soldiers were
given food and drink by their opponents after they sang some of
Euripides' lyrics (Plutarch, *Nicias* 29). Plutarch continues that the
grateful warriors, immediately upon their return to Athens, person-
ally expressed their gratitude to their poetic savior. Plutarch's
Lysander (15.3) preserves a story that, in 404, as Sparta debated
the punishment of the now defeated Athens, its generals stopped
their consideration of civic annihilation and enslavement when they
heard a dinnertime performance of the first choral ode of Euripides'
Electra: "They felt that it would be a barbarous act to annihilate a
city that had produced such men." Now, these later anecdotes
might have been influenced by the heightened prestige of Euripides

in the Hellenistic world (Plutarch lived in the first and second centuries CE), yet they ring reasonably true. But to understand that
popularity and success can be seen very differently than anecdotal
evidence might allow, we need to consider Euripides and the annual
festival for which he composed his dramas, the City Dionysia.

Euripides and the City Dionysia

A resident of a modern city can see a performance of a drama most
weeks, if not most nights of the year, and anyone anywhere can
watch a movie whenever he or she wants. Obviously, an ancient
Athenian did not make regular trips to the cinema, but theater was
not part of his daily life, either. Aeschylus, Sophocles, and Euripides (and Aristophanes) wrote their dramas with the expectation
that they would be performed a single time at the City Dionysia,
the Athenian civic festival held annually in late March in honor of
the god Dionysus. I say they wrote with this *expectation* because
the actual frequency of production is often misunderstood and the
scholarly view of this frequency is currently shifting. Aeschylus
staged his Athenian dramas anew in Sicily, and it is unimaginable
that Euripides, if his trip to Macedonia did occur, did not also produce his older works there. Moreover, sometime during the second
half of the fifth century, posthumous productions of Aeschylean
drama were allowed at the City Dionysia, so Euripides and Sophocles likely composed with this possibility in mind. Vase paintings
from southern Italy frequently depict scenes from Athenian tragedy, which suggests that drama quickly became one of Athens'
most popular exports. On the other hand, the Theater of Dionysus
on the Acropolis was not the only theater in Attica (the term for
greater Athens that included the surrounding countryside), and
scholars increasingly tend to believe that poets, after productions
at the City Dionysia, took their dramas on tour to the smaller the-
aters in the *demes,* the villages that constituted greater Athens.
Nonetheless, the notional, if not actual, sole and "real" production
was for the prestigious competitions of the City Dionysia.

And the Dionysia was extraordinarily competitive, with, among
other things, many contests for choral groups from every tribe of
Athens, and prizes for the best actors and, of course, for the tragic
poet who produced the best slate of dramas, which consisted of
three tragedies and a satyr play (described later in this Introduction). Well before each Dionysia, poets would apply for a chorus to

the archon, the chief magistrate of Athens, who was in charge of all aspects of the festival. The central element in Greek drama was the chorus; because of its size (roughly fifteen for Euripides' career) and the complexity of its theatrical role, a chorus was very expensive to maintain and train for the months of rehearsals, so each one had to be supported by the city and its wealthy citizens. The criteria for the archon's selections remain unknown, though some evidence suggests that a particularly poor showing the previous year could jeopardize an applicant's chances. Because Aristotle's *Poetics* and Aristophanes' *Frogs* (not to mention other sources) name a number of other fifth-century playwrights, it is clear that Euripides would have had to vie for a chorus regularly. In other words, just as a bronze medal in the modern Olympics can obscure the many victories, both national and international, it can take just to reach the final race, so too a third-place finish at the Dionysia hardly suggests abject failure.

In such a competitive (the Greek term is *agonistic*) society, victory garnered its owner considerable glory and prestige, and it is highly unlikely that, in such an environment, disputes over the judging did not arise. Plutarch's *Life of Cimon* (8) tells a story that, when Sophocles won his first victory over Aeschylus, Cimon and several other generals were called on to adjudicate because the spectators had divided among themselves so passionately. The defeated Aeschylus is said to have left then for Sicily, never to return (an apocryphal story that the later production of Aeschylus' *Oresteia* belies). Again, these biographical details can be questioned, but the shape of the story does credibly suggest how high passions might have run. Euripides himself won first prize only three times during his life out of the twenty-two times he competed, and once posthumously (for the program that included the *Bacchae* and *Iphigenia at Aulis*), and human nature would suggest that this rate of success, in the face of Sophocles' eighteen victories, must have rankled him, especially since the events and their judging were so public. We do not know why he won so infrequently, but his stylistic innovations and plot choices probably contributed. It is difficult not to see Medea's complaint (296–305, 304–12 AS) about how clever people are held in suspicion and contempt as to some extent autobiographical. But one must keep in mind that Euripides did reach "the finals"—being thought worthy by the city to receive a chorus—twenty-two times. Many would gladly live with that kind of failure.

The years Euripides did receive a chorus from Athens, he would have participated fully in a most astonishing week of activities: among other events, he would have witnessed or engaged in parades, choral contests, displays of Athenian military power, presentations of civic honor, nine tragedies, three satyr plays, and a number of comedies. Here I summarize the excellent account of the Dionysia from Csapo and Slater's *The Context of Ancient Drama* (1995). All of these events took place at a spring festival in honor of the god Dionysus, a fertility deity who presided over the theater, but whose most prominent symbol was wine. The open-air Theater of Dionysus was located on the south slope of the Athenian Acropolis, a central location that itself indicated the importance of the theatrical festival. The City Dionysia was held in late March, the Athenian month of Elaphebolion, when the onset of milder weather and calmer seas allowed participation from all over the Mediterranean. On the eighth of Elaphebolion, the three poets who had been selected by the archon would appear in the Odeon (at least after its construction around 440), a roofed theater adjacent to the Theater of Dionysus. In the ceremony called the Proagon ("Before the Contest"), the poets would mount a stage, accompanied by their three actors and chorus, wearing garlands but without their costumes and masks. There they would speak about the dramas they were to perform in the coming days. The ninth of Elaphebolion was a day reserved for religious ceremonies, including a procession from the outskirts of Athens into the theater to commemorate the introduction of the god Dionysus to Attica. On the following day, official activities of the city were suspended and the festival began with a parade filled with representatives from all sectors of Athenian society. That same afternoon, there was a competition wherein each of the city's ten tribes would produce a chorus of fifty boys and another of fifty men to perform the choral works known as dithyrambs. As in the performances of tragic dramas, the choral groups would both sing and dance in honor of Dionysus. Thus, because every year 1,000 Athenians would compete in choruses even before the three days of tragic performances, the Theater of Dionysus would be filled with a large group of experts on choral performance, ready to find fault with or praise the choruses of the tragic dramas.

Our sources disagree about what happened on the succeeding days. Many believe that, beginning on the eleventh of Elaphebolion, a day with five comedies was followed by three days in which

each of the approved poets would produce three tragedies and a
satyr play; evidence suggests this was the arrangement before and
after the Peloponnesian War (431–404 BCE), whose economic
hardships likely reduced the number of comic dramas. Another
theory is that there were five days of performances in which comedy and choral competitions were held for two, followed by three
of tragedy and satyr plays. It is clear, however, that the competition
began with a series of ceremonies, including a ritual cleansing of
the theater, libations to the gods poured by generals, the awarding
of golden crowns to prominent citizens who had helped the state
during the previous year, a display of tribute silver sent by subject
members of the Athenian alliance (less charitably called an
empire), and the awarding of armor to orphaned sons of warriors
who had died on behalf of Athens. All of this, and numerous sacrifices of animals, even before a single line was spoken by an actor! It
is thus clear that the performance of Greek drama was woven into
the fabric of Athenian society in a way that would be almost incon-
ceivable for ours.

   To someone of our own time, the most striking feature of each
day of performance might have been the endurance required of
both performers and audience. The performers Euripides had at his
disposal for all of the four plays on his slate were three actors and a
chorus of fifteen; shortly before Euripides' debut, Sophocles had
been allowed to expand the number of actors from two to three.
Those eighteen acted, danced, and sang from very early in the
morning until well into the afternoon. Moreover, even within a single play, each actor had to take several roles, often of wildly different natures; for example, in Euripides' *Hippolytus,* the same actor
played both Phaedra and her husband, Theseus. The simple, realistic masks that the actors donned for each part facilitated this practice. Some actors came to specialize in certain types of roles,
especially those that required the ability to sing the lengthy com-
plex solo arias that Euripides used more and more as his career
progressed. The audience for each day of four plays likely arrived
early, before sunrise, in order to secure the best seats possible on
the stone and wood benches and up onto the bare slope above the
theater itself. Roughly 15,000 Athenians and foreigners thus sat
closely together, an arrangement that must have magnified their
reactions to the emotionally charged events they watched below
them. After performing three tragic dramas that represented love,
death, murder, betrayal, and war, the chorus would return for the

fourth dressed as satyrs, sexually excitable half-man, half-goat creatures, and engage in a burlesque of some sort, possibly parodying the tragedies that preceded them; like tragedy, the satyr dramas drew their plots from Greek mythology. While some need for comic relief after the three tragedies seems understandable, one would be hard-pressed to find an appropriate modern comparison. Perhaps *King Lear* followed by *Monty Python*? While only one pure satyr play survives, Euripides' *Cyclops,* one source tells us that Euripides' first extant work, *Alcestis* (438 BCE), was performed in the place of a satyr play.

Finally, after all of the ceremonies and performances, after the last satyr play on the third day of tragedies, the judges would make their decisions and the winners would be proclaimed before the assembled audience. The victors received a crown of ivy leaves, and then, accompanied by the *choregoi,* the wealthy individuals who had financed their choruses, they were led through the streets of Athens in yet another procession. *Medea,* unfortunately, did not afford Euripides the chance for this extremely happy, and extremely public, celebration.

Euripides and *Medea*

Modern critical attempts to come to grips with Euripidean drama have proven no less contentious than ancient ones seem to have been. Aristophanes aside, quarrels over Euripides began in late-nineteenth-century Europe with Friedrich Nietzsche, who, though better known today as a philosopher, began his career as a classical philologist at the University of Basel. In his short book, *The Birth of Tragedy* (1872), Nietzsche, then infatuated with the operas of Richard Wagner, argued that Greek tragedy had achieved a balance of the two primary forces in the human spirit, the Apollonian (the rational) and the Dionysian (the irrational), until Euripides, with his (alleged) devotion to the philosopher Socrates, tipped the scales in favor of science, thus destroying Greek tragedy. While many believe still that Nietzsche's basic insight into tragic drama was profound, it is difficult to see the author of *Hippolytus* and the *Bacchae* in these criticisms. Nietzsche was immediately, and violently, attacked by his classicist rival, the young Ulrich von Wilamowitz, who then, with a calmer head, proceeded to shape in a fundamental manner the modern study of ancient Greek literature; a defense of the tragedies of Euripides was an essential part of his scholarly career. But conflict has continued through several generations, as Ann Michelini has shown (in Mitchell-Boyask 2002, pp. 51–59). In general, Euripidean scholars advocate one of two main positions: either Euripides was an exponent of traditional Greek values and beliefs, or he was a radical who subjected all aspects of his society to a withering critique. *Medea* seems to offer ammunition for both sides of this split. Do the experiences of Medea expose the oppressiveness of patriarchal Greek culture, or do they affirm every negative Greek stereotype about women? The arguments are as endless as they are rich.

In 431 BCE Euripides offered the audience in the Theater of Dionysus a program consisting of the tragedies *Medea, Philoctetes,* and *Dictys* and the satyr play *Theristae;* of these four plays, only *Medea* survives. So utterly opposite are this drama and its heroine to those of the earlier *Alcestis* that one might be tempted to suggest they were composed as a complementary pair had we not evidence to the contrary: *Medea* was first produced seven years later than *Alcestis,* at the moment when Athens and Sparta girded for war against each other. It is difficult not to imagine that the ferocity of this play's events is related to the tension of that time; a few months after the production of *Medea,* Spartan armies invaded the countryside of Attica, plundering and burning their way to the city walls of Athens, a short walk from the Theater of Dionysus. The world of Athens was changing rapidly, and the savagery unleashed by Euripides in this tragedy seems prophetic of the violence and irrationality that would engulf his civilization in the coming years.

The kernel of this drama's plot, as with *Alcestis,* is simple—a wife's response to her husband's selfishness—and yet Euripides greatly complicates this scenario by making the wife a foreigner and then by continually varying the tone of the marital conflict and his audience's level of sympathy for each side from episode to episode and sometimes even from line to line. The folktale motif of the exotic princess who helps the handsome hero achieve his quest but is callously dispatched by him later is so prevalent in Greek myth that it must have been one of its older story types; Homer seems to play off the expectations of this type of story several times in the *Odyssey.* In Euripides' hands, the relationship has evolved so that the princess is now older, there are children, and the husband, his heroic career over, is dissatisfied with his lot in life. He does not leave her asleep on an island, as Theseus did to Ariadne, but simply takes a new wife, the daughter of the king of Corinth.

The upending of expectations is a fundamental part of Euripides' strategy in this drama. Jason's pursuit of the Golden Fleece had long been one of the central heroic myths of ancient Greece. Sent into exile as a child after Jason's uncle Pelias had deposed Jason's father, Jason had the typical hero's training by the centaur Chiron before returning to Iolcus to reclaim his patrimony. During his absence, he gained the favor of the goddess Hera who already hated Pelias. Pelias sent Jason off to fetch the fleece, officially to prove his worth, but really with the hope that he would not return from the dangerous journey to the Black Sea and the kingdom of Aeëtes, who kept the fleece guarded by a serpent. After assembling a crew of the greatest heroes of the generation before the Trojan War, including Heracles, Jason arrived in Colchis and requested the fleece from Aeëtes, who ordered him to first plow a field with fire-breathing bulls. Aeëtes' teenage daughter Medea, versed in the dark arts and already burning with love for the stranger, anointed his body with a protective oil against the bulls' fire and then put the guardian serpent to sleep. After escaping with the fleece, Medea and Jason killed her young brother, chopping his body to pieces and throwing them, according to various versions, in the palace, overboard, or at Tomis in order to slow the pursuing fleet. Euripides' audience would have known this myth from an early though now lost epic, *Argonautica* (not to be confused with the Hellenistic epic by Apollonius of Rhodes), and from other poems such as Pindar's Fourth Pythian Ode. Euripides himself had dramatized aspects of this legend earlier in his career; as noted above, his very first entry in the City Dionysia included *The Daughters of Pelias*.

But nothing could have prepared his audience for what they saw in 431. As Edith Hall has shown, since the conclusion of the Persian Wars roughly a half-century earlier, Athens had fostered an image of itself as the defender of Greek values, and hence civilization itself, against the barbarians, whose quintessence was the Asiatic Persians; and Medea herself had become a useful symbol for the Persian threat to Greek manhood as embodied by Jason and Theseus. It is possible that the actor (and I stress actor, not actress) who played Medea (and only Medea) wore clothing of a distinctly Persian appearance and a mask that stressed her racial characteristics. A playwright perhaps had no greater challenge than centering a plot on this alien figure, and yet from the drama's opening lines we hear of the perfidy of Jason, the suffering of Medea, and the blind hostility of the Corinthian royal family. The drama thus

explores the legitimacy of the Greek claim to superiority over barbarians. The Chorus of Corinthian women feel more solidarity and
sympathy for Medea as a woman than contempt for her as a barbarian. Medea articulates to them the problems of marriage for
women and the dangers they face in the process of childbirth in an
extraordinary "feminist" speech that tempts us to forget that it was
written by a man and spoken by a man to an audience composed
largely, if not entirely, of men. Jason's self-presentation pushes the
audience's sympathy further toward Medea as he talks in the style
of a Sophist, full of flimsy, glib reasoning and legalisms. Moreover,
as Bernard Knox (1979) observes, Medea's own language about
herself is cast in the idioms of a Homeric warrior, obsessed with
honor and with punishing enemies. Jason's despicable conduct
overshadows whatever warning flags are raised by Medea's clear
manipulation of the men she confronts and by the Nurse's fears
about her dangerous intentions. Euripides manipulates his audience into a position of sympathy for his heroine as skillfully as she
herself manipulates everyone who crosses her path.

Euripides then pulls the rug out from under his audience with
Medea's decision to kill her children. King Aegeus stumbles in on
his way home to Athens after consulting the Delphic oracle concerning his inability to sire children. His willingness to do anything
to help Medea after she promises him assistance with his problem
shows her how overwhelmingly important sons are to men; thus,
she can inflict the maximum pain on Jason by depriving him of his
legacy. She will murder Jason's new bride, and she knows that the
codes of vengeance require that she pay a similar price. The Corin-
thians will kill her sons in response (Jason's first words in the last
scene indicate she is correct in this assumption), so she must do it
first. While the child-murdering Medea is now *the* Medea in our
imagination, it is likely (though not universally agreed among
scholars) that Euripides is the author who created this image; other
ancient sources and the gradual way in which Euripides reveals this
possibility both suggest a transformation of this myth to this most
shocking form. Not only will Medea's actions lead to her children's
deaths, but she herself will be the murderer and will break one of
the most fundamental laws among humans and gods.

But where are the gods? Distant, it seems. Medea is a furious
woman. Jason is a shadow of a hero, with not the least whiff of the
semidivinity of Achilles or Heracles. He has broken his oaths to
Medea, and oaths are sworn to, and thus guaranteed by, the gods.

Jason, who pursues magical objects through fantastical means, seems like a hero from folktale rather than high myth, the realm to which Medea belongs. The Achillean rage of Medea transforms her into something more transcendent, perhaps a form of Hera, the goddess of marriage, the often-betrayed wife of Zeus who had earlier protected Jason but who is in this play nowhere to be seen. Perhaps Medea, in essence, becomes Hera. Anne Burnett (1973) has argued that Medea becomes a quasi-divine personification of the spirit that punishes oath breakers. Medea has continually told her audience that she does the work of the gods in punishing Jason. At the drama's close, she suddenly appears high above the stage, riding on the suspended platform, the space normally used for the gods who often appear late in a tragedy to resolve issues and denounce humans. She flies off to Athens on the dragon-drawn chariot of her grandfather, the sun god Helios. Jason cannot reach her, in either a literal or a figurative sense.

Medea has thus moved from being a sympathetic abused woman, to a monstrous child-killer, and finally to something almost indefinable and incomprehensible: a mother who kills her children and is not only unpunished but actually helped by the gods. Do the gods, then, care more about oaths than the lives of children? Is Euripides thus suggesting that the gods are amoral or, perhaps, ultimately false, uncaring, even unworthy of belief? Has Medea proven her heroic greatness in her punishment of Jason, or has she confirmed every stereotype about women and barbarians that has been articulated by the Greek men in the drama? These are some of the many questions raised at the drama's end. In the City Dionysia of 431, Euripides placed third out of three. I often wonder whether the sheer horror of the deliberate murders of the children had something to do with this defeat.[4]

A Note about Stage Directions

Stage directions are not given in the ancient manuscripts, but here they are based on known theatrical conventions and on signals in the texts. Characters could enter the acting area from the house or from either of the two side entrances. Typically (but not always) the right entrance was used for entrances from the city, and the

---

4. For their comments on a draft of this Introduction, I am grateful to Andromache Karanika, Laura McClure, and Laurialan Reitzammer.

left from nature and the rest of the world; see Wiles (1997). For other concerns with entrances and exits (and sundry aspects of Greek theater practice), see Taplin (1978). For all stage directions in this translation, right and left refer to the audience's spatial orientation.

ROBIN MITCHELL-BOYASK

Translator's Preface

Euripides wrote his plays in highly formal verse whose effects range from natural-sounding conversation in the dialogues to artfully patterned mosaics of sound, sense, and image in the choral odes. The plays are powerful in Greek because the stories are compelling, the language is beautiful, and Euripides had a brilliant eye and ear for the way people act and speak. My goal in bringing this play into English has been to do justice to all of these elements.

The Texts

I have used as my primary text of reference J. Diggle's Oxford Classical Text (*Euripidis Fabulae*, vol. 1, 1984), and have relied heavily on the commentaries of Donald J. Mastronarde and Denys L. Page and on David Kovacs' Loeb Classical Library edition. I have also consulted Anthony J. Podlecki's translation of *Medea*.

The line numbers in the margins are those of my English version; the line numbers of the corresponding Greek text appear in brackets at the top of each page. In this Preface, I cite lines by their numbering in my translation.

The Language

My aim in this translation has been to be faithful to Euripides' sense and to his poetry, with all that each of these involves, including diction, tone, connotation, context, echo, image, euphony, and meter. This endeavor leads to competing claims, of course, and at different times different types of faithfulness have taken precedence over others. As much as possible (given these competing claims), I have sought to translate individual Greek words consistently: for example, *thymos* is always "spirit," and *sôphrosynê* is always "wise restraint" or a variation on that phrase. For keeping track of repetitions, Allen and Italie's *Concordance to Euripides* (1954) has been invaluable. Total consistency in this regard is neither possible nor desirable—a translation that stuck to this principle at all costs would be unreadable—but I have generally been consistent enough to enable students of the play's language and themes to read closely with some confidence. That is, if I repeat an English word, there is a pretty good chance that it reflects a repetition in the Greek, and readers can expect that I have followed any repetitions in the Greek that are thematically significant. A detailed discussion of my practice and principles of translation (especially regarding echoes and repetitions) can be found in my essay "A Translator's Notebook: The Third Stasimon of Euripides' *Hippolytus*," in Richard Armstrong and Elizabeth Vandiver, eds., *Remusings: Classical and Modern Literature* 27.1 (2007).

The Meters

Many elements of the original performances of Euripides' plays are all but lost to us: music and choreography; costumes, masks, and sets; the sound of the actors' voices. What remains in the texts is the poetry, the reason for Euripides' acclaim. All classical Athenian tragedies were written entirely in verse; the closest Euripides comes to prose is the occasional brief interjection, such as "Aaah!" Aside from these, every line is composed with some type of poetic rhythm. Different meters (patterns of heavy and light syllables) were traditional for different parts of each play.

In English, meter is based on patterns of stressed and unstressed syllables. Ancient Greek verse, on the other hand, was "quantitative," based on patterns of long and short syllables; for example, a syllable with the vowel sound "o" as in "hop" was short, and one with "o" as in "hope" was long. Despite this difference in the basis of the English and ancient Greek systems, the patterns themselves— iambic, trochaic, anapestic, dactylic—are comparable, and so it is possible to get some sense of Greek meters through their English analogues. In this translation I have used different English verse rhythms to reflect the changes in meter in the Greek original. These meters fall into three distinct categories, each with its own texture and register: spoken dialogue, anapests (chanted or sung), and lyrics.

Spoken Dialogue

The regular meter for speech in Athenian tragedy was the iambic trimeter. An iamb, in Greek and in English, is a short syllable followed by a long syllable (or unstressed followed by stressed); for example, the word "toDAY" is an iamb. Although the Greek iambic line consists of six iambs, it is called a trimeter because it was treated as three units of two iambs each:

x-LONG-short-LONG—x-LONG-short-LONG—x-LONG-short-LONG

In the "x" (anceps) positions, a long could be substituted for a short. Aristotle said that iambic rhythm was native to everyday Greek speech, and in ordinary conversation people would unintentionally produce lines of iambic verse (*Poetics* 1449a; cf. *Rhetoric* 1408b). The same is true of contemporary English; like ancient Greek, it naturally falls into patterns of alternating light and heavy syllables. I recently received a sample packet of skin lotion with printed instructions that can pass as ordinary prose: "After cleansing and toning, smooth evenly over face. Apply to neck with gentle upward strokes." The second sentence is a perfect iambic pentameter.

The iambic pentameter is the meter I have used wherever Euripides uses iambic trimeter. As the name suggests, it is a line made of five iambs: da-DUM da-DUM da-DUM da-DUM da-DUM. Many variations are traditionally allowed, and I have treated it as essentially a line with five beats.

Anapests

I have used anapestic rhythms wherever Euripides does. An anapest is short-short-LONG, like the word "vioLIN." We tend to associate anapests with comic or children's verse:

> When the Star-Belly Sneetches had frankfurter roasts . . .
> (Dr. Seuss, "The Sneetches")

But anapests have been used in serious English verse as well:

> For the Angel of Death spread his wings on the blast
> (Lord Byron, "The Destruction of Sennacherib")

> Through the gathering darkness, arise . . .
> (Matthew Arnold, "Rugby Chapel: November 1857")

Anapests were used in serious contexts throughout Greek tragedy. They were often used for the exits and entrances of the chorus; they could also be used for passages in a higher emotional register than ordinary speech, or to make a transition between speaking and singing. They were either chanted ("marching anapests") or sung, with slightly different rules defining the two types. In lines 104–204, Medea sings her anapests and the Nurse chants hers; I have used italics to designate the sung parts.

Lyric Meters

The lyric meters, which were sung, have the highest emotional coloring and stand at the greatest distance from ordinary speech. Unlike iambs and anapests, most lyric meters do not translate readily into familiar English equivalents. The most formal lyric passages are the choral odes, which were danced as well as sung. These are organized into pairs of stanzas called "strophe" and "antistrophe," occasionally followed by a third stanza with a different rhythm called an "epode." Any stanza in the text identified with one of these names was set to music and sung.

Strophes and antistrophes always match each other metrically, and the rhythmic repetition was probably emphasized by melodic phrases and dance movements that repeated or mirrored each other. This feature, called "responsion," is the one metrical attribute of Euripides' lyrics that I have consistently attempted to reproduce. For example, the first line of the strophe of the ode that begins at line 1308, "Do you hear the shouts, the shouts of the children?" is matched rhythmically by the first line of the antistrophe, "I've heard of just one, just one other woman" (1323). In this song we also see that lines of iambic spoken dialogue (1310–11, 1315–16) can be incorporated into lyric responsion.

Dochmiacs are a type of lyric meter used to express intense excitement or agitation. They could be used in formal choral odes, for example, at lines 1276–1337, or in lyric dialogue. There were many variations on the dochmiac, whose basic rhythm was short-LONG-LONG-short-LONG. As with all lyric meters, I have not tried to reproduce dochmiacs syllable for syllable, but I have tried to capture their flavor, and I have observed responsion wherever it is found in the texts.

DIANE ARNSON SVARLIEN

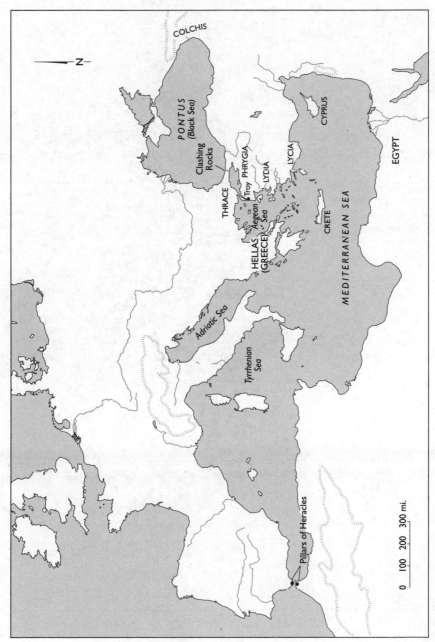

The Ancient Greek World

N

THRACE

BISTONIA

PIERIA
Mt. Olympus △

• Troy

Mt. Ida △

MOLOSSIA
• Dodona

Larissa •

Lake Boebias
△ Mt. Pelion

AEGEAN
SEA

Pherae •

Iolcus

THESSALY

Oechalia (?) •

Delphi •

Thebes •

Eleusis

ISTHMUS

• Athens

Corinth •

Saronic
Gulf

Olympia •

Argos •

Epidaurus •

Tiryns •

• Troezen

PELOPONNESE

• Sparta

NAXOS

IONIAN
SEA

0   30   60 mi

CRETE

Hellas

For My Teachers

Medea

Medea: Cast of Characters

NURSE	of Medea
TUTOR	of Medea and Jason's children
MEDEA	
CHORUS	women of Corinth
CREON	king of Corinth
JASON	
AEGEUS	king of Athens
MESSENGER	
CHILDREN	of Medea and Jason

Medea

SCENE: *A normal house on a street in Corinth. The*
           elderly Nurse steps out of its front door.

NURSE:
I wish the *Argo* never had set sail,
had never flown to Colchis through the dark
Clashing Rocks;[1] I wish the pines had never
been felled along the hollows on the slopes
of Pelion,[2] to fit their hands with oars—   5
those heroes who went off to seek the golden
pelt for Pelias. My mistress then,
Medea, never would have sailed away
to reach the towers of Iolcus' land;[3]
the sight of Jason never would have stunned   10
her spirit with desire. She would have never
persuaded Pelias' daughters to kill their father,
never had to come to this land—Corinth.[4]

---

1. The *Argo* was the ship Jason had constructed with the help of Athena
for his voyage to the Black Sea in order to obtain the Golden Fleece, which
he needed to regain his place as rightful heir to the throne of Iolcus. King
Pelias, who had seized the throne from Jason's father, sent him on this
quest in order to rid himself of Jason when the latter returned from exile.
To reach Colchis, a kingdom on the shore of the Black Sea, the *Argo* had
to sail through the Clashing Rocks, located near the mouth of the
Bosporus. Colchis was the home of Medea.

2. Pelion is a tall mountain in Thessaly, home of the centaur Chiron who
raised Jason during his exile as a baby and youth.

3. Iolcus is a town on the southern coast of Thessaly. Its modern name is
Volo.

4. After Jason returned with the Golden Fleece, Pelias still refused to give
up the throne, so Medea demonstrated to his daughters a spell for restor-
ing their father's youth: she took an old ram, dismembered it, and cooked
its parts in a pot. Out jumped a young ram. Their attempt to perform the
same trick with their father resulted in his death. Euripides' debut in 455
was with a play based on this legend. Jason and Medea then went into exile,

3

Here she's lived in exile with her husband
15   and children, and Medea's presence pleased
the citizens. For her part, she complied
with Jason in all things. There is no greater
security than this in all the world:
when a wife does not oppose her husband.
20   But now, there's only hatred. What should be
most loved has been contaminated, stricken
since Jason has betrayed them—his own children,
and my lady, for a royal bed.
He's married into power: Creon's daughter.⁵
25   Poor Medea, mournful and dishonored,
shrieks at his broken oaths, the promise sealed
with his right hand (the greatest pledge there is)—
she calls the gods to witness just how well
Jason has repaid her. She won't touch food;
30   surrendering to pain, she melts away
her days in tears, ever since she learned
of this injustice. She won't raise her face;
her eyes are glued to the ground. Friends talk to her,
try to give her good advice; she listens
35   the way a rock does, or an ocean wave.
At most, she'll turn her pale neck aside,
sobbing to herself for her dear father,
her land, her home, and all that she betrayed
for Jason, who now holds her in dishonor.
40   This disaster made her realize:
a fatherland is no small thing to lose.
She hates her children, feels no joy in seeing them.
I'm afraid she might be plotting something.⁶

---

eventually reaching Corinth, a prominent city in the northern Peloponnese near the Isthmus. During the year before the production of Euripides' *Medea,* tensions ran high between Athens and Corinth, which then fought against Athens during the Peloponnesian War.

5. This Creon should not be confused with the character in the Oedipus legends. His daughter remains unnamed in this drama.

6. Euripides plants here the germ of the possibility that Medea might harm the children, but it is important to stress that the Nurse fears what Medea might do to others, not to the children. She develops this possibility

Her mind is fierce, and she will not endure
ill treatment. I know her. I'm petrified   45
to think what thoughts she might be having now:
a sharpened knife-blade thrust right through the liver—[i]
she could even strike the royal family, murder
the bridegroom too, make this disaster worse.
[She's a terror. There's no way to be   50
her enemy and come out as the victor.

Here come the children, resting from their games,
with no idea of their mother's troubles.
A child's mind is seldom filled with pain.

> *(Enter the Tutor from the house with the two*
> *children of Jason and Medea.)*

TUTOR:
Timeworn stalwart of my mistress' household,   55
why do you stand here by the gates, alone,
crying out your sorrows to yourself?
You've left Medea alone. Doesn't she need you?

NURSE:
Senior attendant to the sons of Jason,
decent servants feel their masters' griefs   60
in their own minds, when things fall out all wrong.
As for me, my pain was so intense
that a desire crept over me to come out here
and tell the earth and sky my mistress' troubles.

TUTOR:
Poor thing. Is she not done with weeping yet?   65

NURSE:
What blissful ignorance! She's barely started.

TUTOR:
The fool—if one may say such things of masters—
she doesn't even know the latest outrage.

---

at 103, but briefly. Medea's later filicidal intentions must come as a relative
surprise.

NURSE:
What is it, old man? Don't begrudge me that.

TUTOR:
70   Nothing. I'm sorry that I spoke at all.

NURSE:
By your beard, don't hide this thing from *me*,
your fellow-servant. I can keep it quiet.

TUTOR:
As I approached the place where the old men
sit and play dice, beside the sacred spring
75   Peirene,[7] I heard someone say—he didn't
notice I was listening—that Creon,
the ruler of this land, intends to drive
these children and their mother out of Corinth.
I don't know if it's true. I hope it isn't.

NURSE:
80   Will Jason let his sons be so abused,
even if he's fighting with their mother?

TUTOR:
He has a new bride; he's forgotten them.
He's no friend to this household anymore.

NURSE:
We are destroyed, then. Before we've bailed our boat
85   from the first wave of sorrow, here's a new one.

TUTOR:
But please, don't tell your mistress. Keep it quiet.
It's not the time for her to know of this.

NURSE:
Children, do you hear the way your father
is treating you? I won't say, *May he die!*

---

7. Peirene, Corinth's sacred spring, ran down from its acropolis.

—he is my master—but it's obvious   90
he's harming those whom he should love. He's guilty.

TUTOR:
Who isn't? Are you just now learning this,
that each man loves himself more than his neighbor?[ii]
If their father doesn't cherish them, because
he's more preoccupied with his own bed—   95

NURSE:
Go inside now, children. Everything
will be all right.

(The Tutor turns the children toward the house.)

                    And you, keep them away—
don't let them near their mother when she's like this.
I've seen her: she looks fiercer than a bull;
she's giving them the eye, as if she means   100
to do something. Her rage will not let up,
I know, until she lashes out at someone.
May it be enemies she strikes, and not her loved ones!

*(In the following passage, Medea sings and the
Nurse chants.)*

MEDEA:

(From within the house, crying out in rage.)

Aaaah!
Oh, horrible, horrible, all that I suffer,
my unhappy struggles. I wish I could die.   105

NURSE:
You see, this is it. Dear children, your mother
has stirred up her heart, she has stirred up her rage.
Hurry up now and get yourselves inside the house—
but don't get too close to her, don't let her see you:
her ways are too wild, her nature is hateful,   110
her mind is too willful.
                    Go in. Hurry up!

(Exit the Tutor and children into the house.)

It's clear now, it's starting: a thunderhead rising,
swollen with groaning, and soon it will flash
as her spirit ignites it—then what will she do?
115   Her heart is so proud, there is no way to stop her;
her soul has been pierced by these sorrows.

MEDEA:
Aaaah!
The pain that I've suffered, I've suffered so much,
worth oceans of weeping. O children, accursed,
may you die—with your father! Your mother is hateful.
120   *Go to hell, the whole household! Every last one.*

NURSE:
Oh, lord. Here we go. What have *they* done—the children?
Their father's done wrong—why should you hate *them?*
Oh, children, my heart is so sore, I'm afraid
you will come to some harm.
                                        Rulers are fierce
125   in their temperament; somehow, they will not be governed;
they like to have power, always, over others.
They're harsh, and they're stubborn. It's better to live
as an equal with equals. I never would want
to be grand and majestic—just let me grow old
130   in simple security. Even the *word*
"moderation" sounds good when you say it. For mortals
the middle is safest, in word and in deed.
Too much is too much, and there's always a danger
a god may get angry and ruin your household.

(Enter the Chorus of Corinthian women from the
right, singing.)

CHORUS:
135   *I heard someone's voice, I heard someone shout:*
the woman from Colchis: poor thing, so unhappy.
Is her grief still unsoftened? Old woman, please tell us—
I heard her lament through the gates of my hall.
Believe me, old woman, I take no delight
140   *when this house is in pain. I have pledged it my friendship.*

NURSE:
This house? It no longer exists. It's all gone.
He's taken up with his new royal marriage.
She's in her bedroom, my mistress, she's melting
her life all away, and her mind can't be eased
by a single kind word from a single dear friend.   145

MEDEA:
Aaaah!
May a fire-bolt from heaven come shoot through my skull!
What do I gain by being alive?
Oh, god. How I long for the comfort of death.
I hate this life. How I wish I could leave it.

[Strophe]

CHORUS:
Do you hear, O Zeus, O sunlight and earth,   150
this terrible song, the cry
of this unhappy bride?
Poor fool, what a dreadful longing,
this craving for final darkness.
You'll hasten your death. Why do it?   155
Don't pray for this ending.
If your husband reveres a new bed, a new bride,
don't sharpen your mind against him.
You'll have Zeus himself supporting
your case. Don't dissolve in weeping   160
for the sake of your bedmate.

MEDEA:
Great goddess Themis and Artemis, holy one:[8]
do you see what I suffer, although I have bound
my detestable husband with every great oath?
May I see him, along with his bride and the palace   165

---

8. The goddess Themis is a Titan (a member of the first generation of gods
born to Gaia and Ouranos, whose names mean "earth" and "sky") and is
closely associated with Zeus' order and hence with justice and law. The
virgin huntress Artemis, daughter of Zeus, presided over important mat-
ters such as childbirth and life transitions for women.

scraped down to nothing, crushed into splinters.
He started it. He was the one with the nerve
to commit this injustice. Oh father, oh city,
I left you in horror—I killed my own brother.[9]

NURSE:
170   You hear what she says, and the gods that she prays to:
       Themis, and Zeus, the enforcer of oaths?
       There's no way my mistress's rage will die down
       into anything small.

                              [Antistrophe]

CHORUS:
       How I wish she'd come outside, let us see
175   her face, let her hear our words
       and the sound of our voice.
       If only she'd drop her anger,
       unburden her burning spirit,
       let go of this weight of madness.
180   I'll stand by our friendship.
       Hurry up, bring her here, get her out, go inside,
       and bring her to us. Go tell her
       that we are her friends. Please hurry!
       She's raging—the ones inside may
185   feel the sting of her sorrow.

NURSE:
       I'll do as you ask, but I fear that my mistress
       won't listen to me.
       I will make the effort—what's one more attempt?
       But her glare is as fierce as a bull's, let me tell you—
190   she's wild like a lion who's just given birth
       whenever a servant tries telling her anything.

       You wouldn't go wrong, you'd be right on the mark,
       if you called them all half-wits, the people of old:

---

9. To slow down the Colchians who were pursuing Medea and Jason after
the theft of the Golden Fleece, Medea killed her younger brother Apsyrtus
and threw his body parts either around the palace at Colchis or at Tomis
on the shore of the Black Sea.

they made lovely songs for banquets and parties,
but no one took time to discover the music   195
that might do some good, the chords or the harmony
people could use to relieve all the hateful
pain and distress that leads to the downfall
of houses, the deaths and the dreadful misfortunes.
Let me tell you, there would be some gain in that—music   200
with the power to heal. When you're having a sumptuous
feast, what's the point of a voice raised in song?
Why bother with singing? The feast is enough
to make people happy. That's all that they need.

(Exit the Nurse into the house.)

CHORUS:
I heard a wail, a clear cry of pain;   205
she rails at the betrayer of her bed,
the bitter bridegroom.
For the injustice she suffers, she calls on the gods:
Themis of Zeus, protectress of oaths,
who brought her to Hellas, over the salt water dark as night, 210
through the waves of Pontus' forbidding gate.[10]

(Enter Medea from the house, attended by the
Nurse and other female servants. Here spoken
dialogue resumes.)

MEDEA:
Women of Corinth, I have stepped outside
so you will not condemn me. Many people
act superior—I'm well aware of this.
Some keep it private; some are arrogant   215
in public view. Yet there are other people
who, just because they lead a quiet life,
are thought to be aloof. There is no justice
in human eyesight: people take one look
and hate a man, before they know his heart,   220
though no injustice has been done to them.

---

10. Pontus, literally "The Sea," refers to the Black Sea. As the Chorus sing
of the passage through the Bosporus toward Greece, away from her home-
land, Medea passes through the doors of the house.

A foreigner must adapt to a new city,
certainly. Nor can I praise a citizen
who's willful, and who treats his fellow townsmen
225   harshly, out of narrow-mindedness.

My case is different. Unexpected trouble
has crushed my soul. It's over now; I take
no joy in life. My friends, I want to die.
My husband, who was everything to me—
230   how well I know it—is the worst of men.

Of all the living creatures with a soul
and mind, we women are the most pathetic.[11]
First of all, we have to buy a husband:
spend vast amounts of money, just to get
235   a master for our body—to add insult
to injury.[12] And the stakes could not be higher:
will you get a decent husband, or a bad one?
If a woman leaves her husband, then she loses
her virtuous reputation. To refuse him
240   is just not possible. When a girl leaves home
and comes to live with new ways, different rules,
she has to be a prophet—learn somehow
the art of dealing smoothly with her bedmate.
If we do well, and if our husbands bear
245   the yoke without discomfort or complaint,
our lives are admired. If not, it's best to die.
A man, when he gets fed up with the people
at home, can go elsewhere to ease his heart

11. This presentation of the problems of women in marriage is surprising but not unique in Greek tragedy; a surviving fragment of a lost tragedy by Sophocles, *Tereus,* presents a similar lament by Procne, wife of Tereus. After discovering her husband has raped her sister and cut out her tongue, Procne kills their son and serves his flesh to Tereus as a meal. It is unclear which of these two dramas was produced first.

12. Medea here refers to the dowry that the bride's family had to pay to the groom. Divorce, to which she alludes in the succeeding lines, was a relatively easy procedure for men by filing some papers in court, but almost impossibly complicated for women. On the dowry, see Hippolytus' very different complaint at *Hippolytus* 627–29 (688–91 in Arnson Svarlien's translation, hereafter abbreviated AS).

   —he has friends, companions his own age.ⁱⁱⁱ
   We must rely on just one single soul.   250
   They say that we lead safe, untroubled lives
   at home while they do battle with the spear.
   They're wrong. I'd rather take my stand behind
   a shield three times than go through childbirth once.¹³

Still, my account is quite distinct from yours.   255
This is your city. You have your fathers' homes,
your lives bring joy and profit. You have friends.
But I have been deserted and outraged—
left without a city by my husband,
who stole me as his plunder from the land   260
of the barbarians. Here I have no mother,
no brother, no blood relative to help
unmoor me from this terrible disaster.
So, I will need to ask you one small favor.
If I should find some way, some strategy   265
to pay my husband back, bring him to justice,^{iv}
keep silent. Most of the time, I know, a woman
is filled with fear. She's worthless in a battle
and flinches at the sight of steel. But when
she's faced with an injustice in the bedroom,   270
there is no other mind more murderous.

CHORUS:
   I'll do as you ask.¹⁴ You're justified, Medea,
   in paying your husband back. I'm not surprised
   you grieve at your misfortunes.
                   Look! I see Creon,
   the lord of this land, coming toward us now.   275
   He has some new decision to announce.

---

13. The most prominent military tactic in the fifth century BCE was the hop-
lite formation whereby heavily armed soldiers would stand closely together,
moving in a tight formation with shields locked together and spears pointed
forward. Athenian adolescents had to swear an oath to the city in which they
promised, among other things, never to leave their position in the line.

14. A promise by the Chorus not to reveal a protagonist's plan was a frequently used device in order to deal with the awkward situation of having
fifteen people present who could divulge to another character what will
happen. Compare *Hippolytus* 710–12 (786–91 AS).

(Enter Creon from the right, with attendants.)

CREON:
You with the grim face, fuming at your husband,
Medea, I hereby announce that you
must leave this land, an exile, taking with you
280   your two children. You must not delay.
This is my decision. I won't leave
until I've thrown you out, across the border.

MEDEA:
Oh, god. I'm crushed; I'm utterly destroyed.
My enemies, their sails unfurled, attack me
285   and there's no land in sight, there's no escape
from ruin. Although I suffer, I must ask:
Creon, why do you send me from this land?

CREON:
I'll speak plainly: I'm afraid of you.
You could hurt my daughter, even kill her.
290   Every indication points that way.
You're wise[15] by nature, you know evil arts,
and you're upset because your husband's gone
away from your bedroom. I have heard reports
that you've made threats, that you've devised a plan
295   to harm the bride, her father, and the bridegroom.
I want to guard against that. I would rather
have you hate me, woman, here and now,
than treat you gently and regret it later.

MEDEA:
Oh, god.
Creon, this is not the first time: often
300   I've been injured by my reputation.
Any man who's sensible by nature
will set a limit on his children's schooling

---

15. The Greek adjective sophê can mean either "wise" or "clever," and
Greek texts, including this one, often play off of this ambiguity. But
whether the word's connotation here is closer to wise or clever, Euripides
does seem to downplay the traditional representation of Medea as a witch.

to make sure that they never grow too wise.
The wise are seen as lazy, and they're envied
and hated. If you offer some new wisdom   305
to half-wits, they will only think you're useless.
And those who are considered experts hate you
when the city thinks you're cleverer than they are.
I myself have met with this reaction.
Since I am wise, some people envy me,   310
some think I'm idle, some the opposite,ᵛ
and some feel threatened. Yet I'm not all that wise.

And you're afraid of me. What do you fear?
Don't worry, Creon. I don't have it in me
to do wrong to a man with royal power.   315
What injustice have you done to me?
Your spirit moved you, and you gave your daughter
as you saw fit. My husband is the one
I hate. You acted well, with wise restraint.
And now, I don't begrudge your happiness.   320
My best to all of you—celebrate the wedding.
Just let me stay here. I know when I'm beaten.
I'll yield to this injustice. I'll submit
in silence to those greater than myself.

CREON:
Your words are soothing, but I'm terrified   325
of what's in your mind. I trust you less than ever.
⌈It's easier to guard against a woman
│(or man, for that matter) with a fiery spirit
⌊than one who's wise and silent. You must leave
at once—don't waste my time with talk. It's settled.   330
Since you are my enemy, and hate me,
no ruse of yours can keep you here among us.

*(Medea kneels before Creon and grasps his hand
and knees in supplication.)*¹⁶

---

16. Supplication was a ritual act through which an individual abased himself
or herself before a more powerful individual by kneeling and grabbing the
latter's knees, often touching his beard as well. Especially in claiming the pro-
tection of the gods, the supplicant's wish should be granted. Medea makes
little headway here until she calls upon Zeus (341), thus raising the stakes.

MEDEA:
No, by your knees! By your new-married daughter!

CREON:
You're wasting words. There's no way you'll persuade me.

MEDEA:
335   You'll drive me out, with no reverence for my prayers?

CREON:
I care more for my family than for you.

MEDEA:
How clearly I recall my fatherland.

CREON:
Yes, that's what *I* love most—after my children.

MEDEA:
Oh, god—the harm Desire does to mortals!

CREON:
340   Depending on one's fortunes, I suppose.

MEDEA:
Zeus, do not forget who caused these troubles.

CREON:
Just leave, you fool. I'm tired of struggling with you.

MEDEA:
Struggles. Yes. I've had enough myself.

CREON:
My guards will force you out in just a moment.

MEDEA:
345   Oh please, not that! Creon, I entreat you!

CREON:
You intend to make a scene, I gather.

MEDEA:
I'll leave, don't worry. That's not what I'm asking.

CREON:
Why are you forcing me? Let go of my hand!

MEDEA:
Please, let me stay just one more day, that's all.
I need to make arrangements for my exile, 350
find safe asylum for my children, since
their father doesn't give them any thought.
Take pity on them. You yourself have children.
It's only right for you to treat them kindly.
If we go into exile, I'm not worried 355
about myself—I weep for their disaster.

CREON:
I haven't got a ruler's temperament;
reverence has often led me into ruin.
Woman, I realize this is all wrong,
but you shall have your wish. I warn you, though: 360
if the sun god's lamp¹⁷ should find you and your children
still within our borders at first rising,
it means your death. I've spoken; it's decided.
Stay for one day only, if you must.
You won't have time to do the things I fear. 365

*(Exit Creon and attendants to the right. Medea
rises to her feet.)*

CHORUS:
Oh, god! This is horrible, unhappy woman,
the grief that you suffer. Where will you turn?
Where will you findᵛⁱ shelter? What country, what home
will save you from sorrow? A god has engulfed you,
Medea—this wave is now breaking upon you, 370
there is no way out.

---

17. Creon's threat inadvertently includes Helios, Medea's paternal grandfather, who will help her escape at the end of this drama.

MEDEA:
> Yes, things are all amiss. Who could deny it?
> Believe me, though, that's not how it will end.
> The newlyweds have everything at stake,
375 and struggles await the one who made this match.
> Do you think I ever could have fawned
> on him like that without some gain in mind,
> some ruse? I never would have spoken to him,
> or touched him with my hands. He's such an idiot.
380 He could have thrown me out, destroyed my plans;
> instead he's granted me a single day
> to turn three enemies to three dead bodies:
> the father, and the bride, and my own husband.[18] *not the children*
> I know so many pathways to their deaths,
385 I don't know which to turn to first, my friends.
> Shall I set the bridal home on fire,[vii]
> creeping silently into their bedroom?
>
> There's just one threat. If I am apprehended
> entering the house, my ruse discovered,
390 I'll be put to death; my enemies
> will laugh at me.[19] The best way is the most
> direct, to use the skills I have by nature
> and poison them, destroy them with my drugs.
>
> Ah, well.
>
> All right, they die. What city will receive me?
395 What host will offer me immunity,
> what land will take me in and give me refuge?
> There's no one. I must wait just long enough
> to see if any sheltering tower appears.
> Then I will kill in silence, by deceit.
400 But if I have no recourse from disaster,
> I'll take the sword and kill them, even if

---

18. Again, the violence would be directed against Jason, not the children, and the Chorus do not object to actions taken in vengeance against him, Creon, and the bride.

19. Here Medea begins to talk most overtly like a Homeric warrior, obsessed with fame and status, especially in the eyes of "enemies." See Knox, "The *Medea* of Euripides," in Knox (1979), pp. 295–322.

it means my death. I have the utmost nerve.
Now, by the goddess whom I most revere,
Hecate, whom I choose as my accomplice,[20]
who dwells within my inmost hearth, I swear: 405
no one can hurt my heart and then fare well.
I'll turn their marriage bitter, desolate—
they'll regret the match, regret my exile.

And now, spare nothing that is in your knowledge,
Medea: make your plan, prepare your ruse.[21]   410
Do this dreadful thing. There is so much
at stake. Display your courage. Do you see
how you are suffering? Do not allow
these Sisyphean snakes[22] to laugh at you
on Jason's wedding day. Your father is noble;   415
your grandfather is Helios. You have
the knowledge, not to mention woman's nature:
for any kind of noble deed, we're helpless;
for malice, though, our wisdom is unmatched.

CHORUS:

[Strophe 1]

The streams of the holy rivers are flowing backward.   420
Everything runs in reverse—justice is upside down.
Men's minds are deceitful, and nothing is settled,
not even oaths that are sworn by the gods.
The tidings will change, and a virtuous reputation
will grace my name. The race of women will reap   425
honor, no longer the shame of disgraceful rumor.

---

20. The dark goddess Hecate became especially prominent during the fifth century and was associated with witchcraft and magic.

21. Medea talks to herself, an unprecedented event on the Athenian stage (at least in the texts that have survived). This device prepares the audience for her later monologue in which she agonizes over killing her children. See Foley, "Medea's Divided Self," in Foley (2001), pp. 243–71.

22. Sisyphus of Corinth was notorious for his trickery and deceptiveness, for which Zeus punished him in Hades by making him push a boulder up a hill for eternity (*Odyssey* 11.593–600).

[Antistrophe 1]

The songs of the poets of old will no longer linger
on my untrustworthiness. Women were never sent
the gift of divine inspiration by Phoebus
430   Apollo, lord of the elegant lyre,[23]
the master of music—or I could have sung my own song
against the race of men. The fullness of time
holds many tales: it can speak of both men and women.

[Strophe 2]

You sailed away from home and father,
435   driven insane in your heart; you traced a path
between the twin cliffs of Pontus.
The land you live in is foreign.
Your bed is empty, your husband
gone. Poor woman, dishonored,
440   sent into exile.

[Antistrophe 2]

The Grace of oaths is gone, and Reverence
flies away into the sky, abandoning
great Hellas. No father's dwelling
unmoors you now from this heartache.
445   Your bed now yields to another:
now a princess prevails,
greater than you are.

(Enter Jason from the right.)

JASON:
This is not the first time—I have often
observed that a fierce temper is an evil
450   that leaves you no recourse. You could have stayed
here in this land, you could have kept your home

---

23. The epithet *Phoebus* means "shining." Apollo is the leader of the
Muses, the goddesses of music and poetry. The Chorus, of course, ignore
Sappho, a real poetess who would have been unknown to a fictional group
in a story set in the heroic age.

by simply acquiescing in the plans
of those who are greater. You are now an exile
because of your own foolish words. To me
it makes no difference. You can keep on calling   455
Jason the very worst of men.²⁴ However,
the words you spoke against the royal family—
well, consider it a gain that nothing worse
than exile is your punishment. As for me,
I wanted you to stay. I always tried   460
to calm the king, to soothe his fuming rage.
But you, you idiot, would not let up
your words against the royal family. That's why
you are now an exile. All the same,
I won't let down my loved ones. I have come here   465
looking out for your best interests, woman,
so you won't be without the things you need
when you go into exile with the children.
You'll need money—banishment means hardship.
However much you hate me, I could never   470
wish you any harm.

MEDEA:
               You are the worst!
You're loathsome—that's the worst word I can utter.
You're not a man. You've come here—most detested
by the gods, by me, by all mankind.ᵛⁱⁱⁱ
That isn't courage, when you have the nerve   475
to harm your friends, then look them in the face.
No, that's the worst affliction known to man:
shamelessness.
             And yet, I'm glad you've come.
Speaking ill to you will ease my soul,
and listening will cause you pain. I'll start   480
at the beginning. First, I saved your life—
as every single man who sailed from Hellas
aboard the *Argo* knows—when you were sent

---

24. Variations on "worst of men" recur throughout this scene. It inverts
the hero's traditional desire to be called "the best." In the epics of the Trojan War, all heroes vied for this title, often, as in the case of Ajax, at the
cost of their lives.

to yoke the fire-breathing bulls, and sow
485   the deadly crop. I killed the dragon, too:
the sleepless one, who kept the Golden Fleece
enfolded in his convoluted coils;[25]
I was your light, the beacon of your safety.
For my part, I betrayed my home, my father,
490   and went with you to Pelion's slopes, Iolcus—
with more good will than wisdom—and I killed
Pelias, in the cruelest possible way:
at his own children's hands. I ruined their household.

And you—you *are* the very worst of men—
495   betrayed me, after all of that. You wanted
a new bed, even though I'd borne you children.
If you had still been childless, anyone
could understand your lust for this new marriage.

All trust in oaths is gone. What puzzles me
500   is whether you believe those gods (the ones
who heard you swear) no longer are in power,
or that the old commandments have been changed?
You realize full well you broke your oath.

Ah, my right hand, which you took so often,
505   clinging to my knees. What was the point
of touching me?[26] You are despicable.
My hopes have all gone wrong. Well, then! You're here:
I have a question for you, friend to friend.
(What good do I imagine it will do?
510   Still, I'll ask, since it makes you look worse.)
Where do I turn now? To my father's household

---

25. When Jason asked Medea's father, King Aeëtes, for the fleece, he was
required to yoke these bulls (Medea gave Jason a magic lotion to protect
him from the fire) and sow the ground with the teeth of the serpent Cadmus had killed at the foundation of Thebes. From these teeth sprang
armed men. It is unclear how Medea killed the dragon, and other versions
of the story do not credit her with the actual killing. A vase painting in the
Vatican collection shows Jason half-swallowed by the dragon, with Athena, protector of heroes, standing by watching.

26. In other words, Jason claimed supplication but then ignored his part
of the reciprocal relationship. Oaths were sworn to the gods. To disregard
oaths was thus to commit an offense against the gods.

and fatherland, which I betrayed for you?
Or Pelias' poor daughters? Naturally
they'll welcome me—the one who killed their father!

Here is my situation. I've become   515
an enemy to my own family, those
whom I should love, and I have gone to war
with those whom I had no reason at all
to hurt, and all for your sake. In exchange,
you've made me the happiest girl in all of Hellas.   520
I have you, the perfect spouse, a marvel,
so trustworthy—though I must leave the country
friendless and deserted, taking with me
my friendless children! What a charming scandal
for a newlywed: your children roam   525
as beggars, with the one who saved your life.ix

Zeus! For brass disguised as gold, you sent us
reliable criteria to judge.
But when a man is base, how can we know?
Why is there no sign stamped upon his body?²⁷   530

CHORUS:
    This anger is a terror, hard to heal,
    when loved ones clash with loved ones in dispute.

JASON:
    It seems that I must have a way with words
    and, like a skillful captain, reef my sails
    in order to escape this gale that blows   535
    without a break—your endless, tired harangue.
    The way I see it, woman (since you seem
    to feel that I must owe you some huge favor),
    it was Cypris,²⁸ no other god or mortal,
    who saved me on my voyage. Yes, your mind   540
    is subtle. But I must say—at the risk

---

27. The fifth century BCE saw an increasing concern with the discrepancy
between external appearance and internal human nature. See, e.g., similar
concerns at *Hippolytus* 925–31 (1028–37 AS).

28. Aphrodite is called Cypris because, after her birth in the sea, she came
ashore on the island of Cyprus.

of stirring up your envy and your grudges—
Eros was the one who forced your hand:
his arrows, which are inescapable,
545   compelled you to rescue me. But I won't put
too fine a point on that. You *did* support me.
You saved my life, in fact. However, you
received more than you gave, as I shall prove.[29]
First of all, you live in Hellas now
550   instead of your barbarian land. With us,
you know what justice is, and civil law:[30]
not mere brute force. And every single person
in Hellas knows that you are wise. You're famous.
You'd never have that kind of reputation
555   if you were living at the edge of nowhere.
As for me, I wouldn't wish for gold
or for a sweeter song than Orpheus'[31]
unless I had the fame to match my fortune.

Enough about my struggles—you're the one
560   who started this debate. As for my marriage
to the princess, which you hold against me,
I shall show you how I acted wisely
and with restraint, and with the greatest love
toward you and toward our children—Wait! Just listen![32]
565   When I moved here from Iolcus, bringing with me

---

29. The self-consciously rhetorical style of Jason here would have reminded the audience of the Sophists, the teachers of rhetoric who were prevalent in Athens during these decades. The association would not have been a positive one.

30. Jason ignores that oaths are foundational to a society bound by law. His linkage of lawfulness to Hellenism thus raises the question of who the real "barbarian" is.

31. The son of Apollo and a Muse, Orpheus was a singer with almost miraculous powers. He served as one of Jason's Argonauts. Orpheus was also willing to travel to Hades to ask Hades and Persephone (Demeter's daughter) for the return of his wife Eurydice, who had been killed by a snake bite. Charmed by his songs, they agreed, on the condition that Orpheus not look back at Eurydice until he and his wife reached the surface of the earth. He could not resist looking back, and she returned to the dead.

32. This interjection indicates that Medea must react physically to this outlandish claim.

disaster in abundance, with no recourse,
what more lucky windfall could I find
(exile that I was) than marrying
the king's own child? It's not that I despised
your bed—the thought that irritates you most—   570
nor was I mad with longing for a new bride,
or trying to compete with anyone—
to win the prize for having the most children.
I have enough—no reason to complain.
My motive was the best: so we'd live well   575
and not be poor. I know that everyone
avoids a needy friend. I wanted to raise
sons in a style that fits my family background,
give brothers to the ones I had with you,
and treat them all as equals. This would strengthen   580
the family, and I'd be blessed with fortune.
What do *you* need children for? For me, though,
it's good if I can use my future children
to benefit my present ones. Is that
bad planning? If you weren't so irritated   585
about your bed, you'd never say it was.
But you're a woman—and you're all the same!
If everything goes well between the sheets
you think you have it all. But let there be
some setback or disaster in the bedroom   590
and suddenly you go to war against
the things that you should value most. I mean it—
men should really have some other method
for getting children. The whole female race
should not exist. It's nothing but a nuisance.[33]   595

CHORUS:
    Jason, you've composed a lovely speech.
    But I must say, though you may disagree:
    you have betrayed your wife. You've been unjust.

---

33. Compare *Hippolytus* 618–24 (680–87 AS). While the ideology of
Greek society was patriarchal and in many senses misogynistic, it is inter-
esting that, at least in Athenian tragic drama, men who make such state-
ments wind up destroyed. On the capacity of the "multivocal" form of
Greek tragedy to overcome the limitations of its society, see Edith Hall,
"The Sociology of Greek Tragedy," in Easterling (1997), pp. 93–126.

MEDEA:
Now, this is where I differ from most people.
600   In my view, someone who is both unjust
and has a gift for speaking—such a man
incurs the greatest penalty. He uses
his tongue to cover up his unjust actions,
and this gives him the nerve to stop at nothing
605   no matter how outrageous. Yet he's not
all that wise. Take your case, for example.

Spare me this display of cleverness;
a single word will pin you to the mat.
If you weren't in the wrong, you would have told me
610   your marriage plans, not kept us in the dark—
your loved ones, your own family!

JASON:
                                        Yes, of course
you would have been all for it! Even now
you can't control your rage against the marriage.

MEDEA:
That's not what you were thinking. You imagined
615   that for an older man, a barbarian wife
was lacking in prestige.

JASON:
                                        No! Please believe me:
It wasn't for the woman's sake I married
into the king's family. As I have said,
I wanted to save you, and give our children
620   royal brothers, a safeguard for our household.

MEDEA:
May I not have a life that's blessed with fortune
so painful, or prosperity so irritating.

JASON:
Your prayer could be much wiser: don't consider
what's useful painful. When you have good fortune,
don't see it as a hardship.

MEDEA:

                    Go ahead—   625
    you have somewhere to turn!—commit this outrage.
    I am deserted, exiled from this land.

JASON:
    You brought that on yourself. Don't blame another.

MEDEA:
    Did I remarry? How did I betray you?

JASON:
    You blasphemously cursed the royal family.   630

MEDEA:
    And I'm a curse to your family as well.   .

JASON:
    I won't discuss this with you any further.   .
    If you'd like me to help you and the children   .
    with money for your exile, then just say so.   .
    I'm prepared to give with an open hand,   635
    and make arrangements with my friends to show you .
    hospitality. They'll treat you well.   .
    You'd be an idiot to refuse this offer.   .
    You'll gain a lot by giving up your anger.   .

MEDEA:
    ⌈I wouldn't stay with your friends, and I would never . 640
    │accept a thing from you. Don't even offer.   .
    ⌊There is no profit in a bad man's gift.   .

JASON:
    All the same, I call the gods to witness: .
    I only want to help you and the children.   .
    But you don't want what's good; you push away   645
    your friends; you're willful. And you'll suffer for it.   ·

MEDEA:
    Get out of here. A craving for your new bride
    has overcome you—you've been away so long.

650   Go, celebrate your wedding. It may be
          (the gods will tell) a marriage you'll regret.

              (Exit Jason to the right.)

CHORUS:

                    [Strophe 1]

          Desire, when it comes on too forcefully, never bestows
          excellence, never makes anyone prestigious.
          When she comes with just the right touch, there's no goddess
              more gracious
          than Cypris.
655   Mistress, never release from your golden bow
          an inescapable arrow, smeared with desire
          and aimed at my heart.

                    [Antistrophe 1]

          Please, let me be cherished by Wisdom, be loved by Restraint,
          loveliest gift of the gods. May dreadful Cypris
660   never stun my spirit with love for the bed of another
          and bring on
          anger, battles of words, endless fighting, strife.
          Let her be shrewd in her judgment; let her revere
          the bedroom at peace.

                    [Strophe 2]

665   O fatherland, O home, never allow
          me to be without a city:
          a grief without recourse, life that's hard to live through,
          most distressing of all fates.
          May I go to my death, my death
670   before I endure that; I'd rather face
          my final day. There's no worse heartache
          than to be cut off from your fatherland.

                    [Antistrophe 2]

          We've seen it for ourselves; nobody else
          gave me this tale to consider.
675   No city, no friend will treat you with compassion

in your dreadful suffering.
May he die, the ungracious man
who won't honor friends, who will not unlock
his mind to clear, calm thoughts of kindness.
I will never call such a man my friend.   680

(Enter Aegeus from the left.) [34]

AEGEUS:
Medea, I wish all the best to you.
There is no finer way to greet a friend.

MEDEA:
All the best to you, Aegeus, son
of wise Pandion. Where are you traveling from?

AEGEUS:
I've come from Phoebus' ancient oracle. [35]   685

MEDEA:
What brought you to the earth's prophetic navel?

AEGEUS:
Seeking how I might beget a child.

MEDEA:
By the gods, are you still childless?

---

34. Aegeus' is the only entrance from the left in the entire play, which underscores the unexpectedness of his arrival. Aegeus, son of Pandion, is one of the early kings of Athens. He has been visiting the oracle at Delphi in order to learn the cause of his childlessness. A vase painting now in Berlin depicts Aegeus consulting the goddess Themis at Delphi. The son promised at this visit will turn out to be Theseus. In a tragedy that did not survive antiquity, *Theseus,* Euripides dramatized the story of Theseus' arrival at Athens and the attempt by Medea to kill him because she believed him to be a threat to her position.

35. Apollo's mountainside oracle at Delphi was the most prominent center of prophecy in the Greek world. Sterility was a frequent cause for inquiries by pilgrims there. The "navel" mentioned by Medea is the *omphalos,* the "navel stone," believed to mark the center of the earth, which was kept on display at Delphi.

AEGEUS:
Still childless. Some god must be to blame.

MEDEA:
690   Do you have a wife, or do you sleep alone?

AEGEUS:
I'm married, and we share a marriage bed.

MEDEA:
Well, what did Phoebus say concerning children?

AEGEUS:
His words were too profound for human wisdom.

MEDEA:
May I hear the oracle? Is it permitted?

AEGEUS:
695   Yes, why not? This calls for a wise mind.

MEDEA:
Then tell me, if indeed it is permitted.

AEGEUS:
He said, "Don't loose the wineskin's hanging foot . . ."[36]

MEDEA:
Before you do what thing? Or reach what place?

AEGEUS:
Before returning to my paternal hearth.

MEDEA:
700   And why have you sailed here? What do you need?

---

36. The leg of the animal-skin wine bag was tied up and then loosened as a spigot for dispensing wine. This phallic image lends itself to a prophecy of the appropriate time for successful intercourse.

AEGEUS:
There is a man named Pittheus, lord of Troezen . . .[37]

MEDEA:
Pelops' son. They say he's very pious.[38]

AEGEUS:
I want to bring this prophecy to him.

MEDEA:
Yes. He's wise, and well-versed in such things.

AEGEUS:
And most beloved of my war companions.   705

MEDEA:
Good luck to you. May you get what you desire.

AEGEUS:
But you—your eyes are melting. What's the matter?

MEDEA:
My husband is the very worst of men.

AEGEUS:
What are you saying? Why the low spirits? Tell me.

MEDEA:
Jason treats me unjustly. I've done him no harm.   710

AEGEUS:
What has he done? Explain to me more clearly.

---

37. Pittheus, who understands the prophecy, gives his daughter Aethra
to Aegeus after getting him drunk. After Theseus is born at Troezen, he is
raised by his mother and Pittheus, who later also raises Theseus' son
Hippolytus.

38. Pelops was the son of Tantalus, served by his father as a meal to the
gods. After his life was restored, he became the heroic founder of the
southern peninsula of Greece, which was then named the Peloponnese,
"the island of Pelops," after him.

MEDEA:
He has another wife, who takes my place.

AEGEUS:
No. He wouldn't dare. It's much too shameful.

MEDEA:
It's true. His former loved ones are dishonored.

AEGEUS:
715   Did he desire another? Or tire of you?

MEDEA:
Oh yes, he felt desire. We cannot trust him.

AEGEUS:
Let him go, if he's as bad as you say.

MEDEA:
He desired a royal marriage-bond.

AEGEUS:
Who's giving away the bride? Go on, continue.

MEDEA:
720   Creon, the ruler of this land of Corinth.

AEGEUS:
Woman, your pain is understandable.

MEDEA:
I am destroyed. And that's not all—I'm exiled.

AEGEUS:
By whom? This is new trouble on top of trouble.

MEDEA:
By Creon. He is driving me from Corinth.

AEGEUS:
725   And Jason is allowing it? Shame on him.

MEDEA:
He claims to be against it, but he'll manage
to endure it somehow.

(Medea again assumes the supplicant position.)

Listen, I entreat you;
by your beard and by your knees, I beg you:
Have pity on me; pity my misfortune.
Don't let me go deserted into exile;   730
receive me in your home and at your hearth.
If you do it, may the gods grant your desire
for children; may you die a prosperous man.
You don't know what a windfall you have found!
I'll cure your childlessness, make you a father.   735
I know the drugs required for such things.

AEGEUS:
For many reasons, woman, I am eager
to grant this favor to you: first, the gods;
and secondly, the children that you promise.
I'm at a total loss where that's concerned.   740
But this is how it is. When you arrive,
I'll treat you justly, try to shelter you.
However, you must know this in advance:
I'm not willing to escort you from this land.
If you can come to my house on your own,   745
I'll let you stay there—it will be your refuge.
I will not give you up to anyone.
But you must leave this land all by yourself.
My hosts here must have no complaint with me.

MEDEA:
So be it. But if I had some assurance   750
that I could trust you, I'd have all I need.

AEGEUS:
You don't believe me? Tell me, what's the problem?

MEDEA:
Oh, I believe you. But I have enemies:

Creon, and the house of Pelias.
755   If they come for me, and you're not bound
        by any oath, then you might let them take me.
        A promise in words only, never sworn
        by any gods, might not be strong enough
        to keep you from befriending them, from yielding
760   to their delegations. I'm completely helpless;
        they have prosperity and royal power.

AEGEUS:
        Your words show forethought. If you think it's best,
        I'll do it without any hesitation.
        In fact, this is the safest course for me:
765   I'll have a good excuse to turn away
        your enemies. And things are settled well
        for you, of course. I'll swear: just name the gods.

MEDEA:
        ⌈Swear by the Earth we stand on, and by Helios—
        ⌊my father's father—and the whole race of gods.

AEGEUS:
770   To do or not do what? Just say the word.

MEDEA:
        Never to expel me from your land yourself,
        and never, as long as you live, to give me up
        willingly to any enemy.

AEGEUS:
        I swear by Earth, by Helios' sacred light,
775   by all the gods: I'll do just as you say.

MEDEA:
        Fine. And if you don't? What would you suffer?

AEGEUS:
        Whatever an unholy man deserves.

        (Medea rises.)

MEDEA:

Fare well, then, on your voyage. This is good.
I'll find you in your city very soon,
once I've done my will, and had my way. 780

(Exit Aegeus to the left. The Chorus address him
as he leaves.)

CHORUS:

May lord Hermes, the child of Maia, escort you[39]
and bring you back home. May you do as you please,
and have all you want. In my judgment, Aegeus,
you're a good, noble man.

MEDEA:

O Zeus, and Zeus's Justice, and the light 785
of Helios, I now shall be the victor
over my enemies. My friends, I've set my foot
upon the path. My enemies will pay
what justice demands—I now have hope of this.
This man, when I was at my lowest point, 790
appeared, the perfect harbor for my plans.
When I reach Pallas' city,[40] I shall have
a steady place to tie my ship. And now
I'll tell you what my plans are. Hear my words;
they will not bring you pleasure. I will send 795
a servant to bring Jason here to see me.
When he comes, I'll soothe him with my words:
I'll say that I agree with him, that he
was right to marry into the royal family,
betraying me—well done, and well thought out! 800
"But let my children stay here!" I will plead—
not that I would leave them in this land
for my enemies to outrage—my own children.
No: this is my deceit, to kill the princess.
I'll send them to her, bearing gifts in hand^x 805
—a delicate robe, and a garland worked in gold.

---

39. Hermes, divine son of Zeus and the nymph Maia, is the protector of
travelers.
40. Medea refers to Athens here. *Pallas* is one of Athena's epithets.

If she takes these fine things and puts them on,
she, and anyone who touches her,
will die a painful death. Such are the drugs
with which I will smear them.
810   But enough of that.
⌈Once that's done, the next thing I must do
│chokes me with sorrow. I will kill the children—
⌊my children. No one on this earth can save them.
I'll ruin Jason's household, then I'll leave
815   this land, I'll flee the slaughter of the children
I love so dearly. I will have the nerve
for this unholy deed. You see, my friends,
I will not let my enemies laugh at me.

Let it go. What do I gain by being alive?
820   I have no fatherland, no home, no place
to turn from troubles. The moment I went wrong
was when I left my father's house, persuaded
by the words of that Greek man. If the gods will help me,
he'll pay what justice demands. He'll never see
825   them alive again, the children that I bore him.
Nor will he ever father another child:
his new bride, evil woman, she must die
an evil death, extinguished by my drugs.
Let no one think that I'm a simpleton,
830   or weak, or idle—I am the opposite.
I treat my friends with kindness, and come down hard
on the heads of my enemies. This is the way to live,
the way to win a glorious reputation.[41]

CHORUS:
    Since you have brought this plan to us, and since
835   I want to help you, and since I support
    the laws of mankind, I ask you not to do this.

MEDEA:
    There is no other way. It's understandable
    that you would say this—you're not the one who's suffered.

_____

41. Jason has destroyed Medea's identity as a wife. She now in return can-
cels her maternity, and as part of this process the shift to the language of
the male warrior has begun to accelerate over the course of this speech.

CHORUS:
Will you have the nerve to kill your children?

MEDEA:
Yes: to wound my husband the most deeply.   840

CHORUS:
And to make yourself the most miserable of women.

MEDEA:
Let it go. Let there be no more words
until it's done.

(To her attendant.)

You: go now, and bring Jason.
When I need to trust someone, I turn to you.
If you're a woman and mean well to your mistress,   845
do not speak of the things I have resolved.

(Exit the attendant to the right.)

CHORUS:

[Strophe 1]
The children of Erechtheus[42] have always prospered,
descended from blessèd gods.
They graze, in their sacred stronghold, on glorious wisdom,
with a delicate step through the clear and brilliant air.   850
They say that there
the nine Pierian Muses[43] once gave birth
to Harmony with golden hair.

---

42. Athenians. Erechtheus was a legendary early king of Athens. His temple, the Erechtheum, was one of the two most prominent buildings on the Acropolis.
43. The Muses are the children of Zeus and Mnemosynê. Pieria, an important center of worship to the Muses, was often said to be their birthplace.

[Antistrophe 1]

They sing that Cypris dipped her pitcher in the waters
855   of beautiful Cephisus;[44]
she sighed, and her breaths were fragrant and temperate breezes.
With a garland of sweet-smelling roses in her hair
she sends Desires
to take their places alongside Wisdom's throne
860   and nurture excellence with her.

[Strophe 2]

How can this city
of holy rivers,
receiver of friends and loved ones,
receive you—when you've murdered your own children,
865   most unholy woman—among them?
Just think of this deathblow aimed at the helpless,
think of the slaughter you'll have on your hands.
Oh no, by your knees, we beg you,
we beg you, with every plea
870   we can plead: do not kill your children.

[Antistrophe 2]

Where will you find it,
the awful courage?
The terrible nerve—how can you?
How can your hand, your heart, your mind go through with
875   this slaughter? How will you be able
to look at your children, keep your eyes steady,
see them beseech you, and not fall apart?
Your tears will not let you kill them;
your spirit, your nerve will fail:
880   you will not soak your hands in their blood.

(Enter Jason from the right.)

JASON:
I've come because you summoned me. Despite

---

44. Cephisus is one of the two main rivers in Athens.

the hate between us, I will hear you out.
What is it this time, woman? What do you want?

MEDEA:
Jason, I beg you, please forgive the things
I said. Your heart should be prepared, receptive   885
like a seed bed. We used to love each other.
It's only right for you to excuse my anger.
I've thought it over, and I blame myself.
Pathetic! Really, I must have been insane
to stand opposed to those who plan so well,   890
to be an enemy to those in power
and to my husband, who's done so well by me:
marrying the royal princess, to beget
brothers for my children. Isn't it time
to drop my angry spirit, since the gods   895
have been so bountiful? What's wrong with me?
Don't I have children? Aren't we exiles? Don't we
need whatever friendship we can get?
That's what I said to myself. I realize
that I've been foolish, that there is no point   900
to all my fuming rage. I give you credit
for wise restraint, for making this connection,
this marriage that's in all our interests. Now
I understand that you deserve my praise.
I was such a moron. I should have supported   905
your plans, I should have made arrangements with you,
I should have stood beside the bridal bed,
rejoiced in taking care of your new bride.

We women—oh, I won't say that we're bad,
but we are what we are. You shouldn't sink   910
down to our level, trading childish insults.
I ask for your indulgence. I admit
I wasn't thinking straight, but now my plans
are much improved where these things are concerned.

> *(Medea turns toward the house to call the
> children.)*

Oh, children! Come out of the house, come here,   915
come out and greet your father, speak to him.

Come set aside, together with your mother,
the hatred that we felt toward one we love.

*(The children come out from the house, escorted
by the Tutor and attendants.)*

We've made a treaty. My rage has gone away.
Take his right hand.

920   Oh, god, my mind is filled
with bad things, hidden things. Oh, children, look—
your lovely arms, the way you stretch them out.
Will you look this way your whole long lives?
I think I'm going to cry. I'm filled with fear.
925   After all this time, I'm making up
my quarrel with your father. This tender sight
is washed with tears; my eyes are overflowing.

CHORUS:
In my eyes too fresh tears are welling up.
May this evil not go any further.

JASON:
930   Woman, I approve your new approach—
not that I blame you for the way you felt.
It's only right for a female to get angry
if her husband smuggles in another wife.
But this new change of heart is for the best.
935   After all this time, you've recognized
the winning plan. You're showing wise restraint.
And as for you, my children, you will see
your father is no fool. I have provided
for your security, if the gods will help me.
940   Yes, I believe that you will be the leaders
here in Corinth, with your future brothers.
Grow up strong and healthy. All the rest
your father, with the favor of the gods,
will take care of. I pray that I may see you
945   grown up and thriving, holding sway above
my enemies.

(Jason turns to Medea.)

You! Why have you turned
your face away, so pale? Why are fresh tears
pouring from your eyes? Why aren't you happy
to hear what I have had to say?

MEDEA:

                               It's nothing.
I was only thinking of the children.   950

JASON:
Don't worry now. I'll take good care of them.

MEDEA:
I'll do as you ask. I'll trust in what you say.
I'm female, that's all. Tears are in my nature.

JASON:
So—why go on? Why moan over the children?

MEDEA:
They're mine. And when you prayed that they would live,   955
pity crept over me. I wondered: would they?
As for the things you came here to discuss,
we've covered one. I'll move on to the next.
Since the royal family has seen fit
to exile me (and yes, I realize   960
it's for the best—I wouldn't want to stay
to inconvenience you, or this land's rulers,
who see me as an enemy of the family),
I will leave this land, go into exile,
but you must raise your children with your own hand: 965
ask Creon that they be exempt from exile.

JASON:
Though I may not persuade him, I must try.

MEDEA:
And ask your wife to ask her father: please
let the children be exempt from exile.

JASON:
970   Certainly. I think I will persuade her.

MEDEA:
No doubt, if she's a woman like all others.
And for this work, I'll lend you my support.
I'll send her gifts, much lovelier, I know,
than any living person has laid eyes on:
975   a delicate robe, and a garland worked in gold.[45]
The children will bear them. Now, this very minute,
let one of the servants bring these fine things here.

> *(An attendant goes into the house to carry out this request. She, or another servant, returns with the finery.)*

She will be blessed a thousandfold with fortune:
with you, an excellent man to share her bed,
980   and these possessions, these fine things that once
my father's father, Helios, passed down
to his descendants. Take these wedding gifts
in your arms, my children; go and give them
to the lucky bride, the royal princess.
985   These are gifts that no one could find fault with.

> *(The attendant puts the gifts in the children's arms.)*

JASON:
You fool! Why let these things out of your hands?
Do you think the royal household needs more robes,
more gold? Hold onto these. Don't give them up.
If my wife thinks anything of me,
990   I'm sure that I mean more to her than wealth.

---

45. Gold here evokes the Golden Fleece. Medea would destroy her rival with a token that reminds all of how Jason first won Medea. Spinning and weaving were, moreover, the activities of the good wife, and Medea here, like Clytemnestra, uses fabric as the lethal symbol of the dissolution of her marriage. In Aeschylus' *Oresteia* (*Agamemnon* 905–57), Clytemnestra spreads out a rich tapestry before Agamemnon and convinces him to walk on it. She thus proves, among other things, his arrogance.

MEDEA:
Don't say that. Even the gods can be persuaded
by gifts. And gold is worth a thousand words.
She has the magic charm; the gods are helping
her right now: she's young, and she has power.
To save my children from exile, I'd give my life,   995
not merely gold. You, children, when you've entered
that wealthy house, must supplicate your father's
young wife, my mistress. You must plead with her
and ask her that you be exempt from exile.
Give her these fine things. That is essential: 1000
she must receive these gifts with her own hands.
Go quickly now, and bring back to your mother
the good news she desires—that you've succeeded.

*(The children, bearing the gifts, leave with the
Tutor to the right.)*

CHORUS:

[Strophe 1]

Now I no longer have hope that the children will live,
no longer. They walk to the slaughter already.   1005
The bride will receive the crown of gold;
she'll receive her horrible ruin.
Upon her golden hair, with her very own hands,
she'll place the fine circlet of Hades.

[Antistrophe 1]

She'll be persuaded; the grace and the heavenly gleam   1010
will move her to try on the robe and the garland.
The bride will adorn herself for death.
for the shades below. She will fall
into this net; her death will be horrible. Ruin
will be inescapable, fated.   1015

[Strophe 2]

And you, poor thing, bitter bridegroom, in-law to royalty:
you don't know you're killing your children,
bringing hateful death to your bride.
How horrible: how unaware you are of your fate.

[Antistrophe 2]

1020   I cry for your pain in turn, poor thing; you're a mother, yet
you will slaughter them, your own children,
for the sake of your bridal bed,
the bed that your husband now shares with somebody else.

*(The Tutor returns, at the right, from the palace
with the children.)*

TUTOR:
Mistress, your children are released from exile.
1025   The princess happily received the gifts
with her own hands. As far as she's concerned,
the children's case is settled; they're at peace.

Ah!
Why are you upset by your good fortune?[xi]

MEDEA:
Oh, god.

TUTOR:
              Your cry is out of tune. This is good news!

MEDEA:
Oh god, oh god.

TUTOR:
1030   Have I made some mistake?
Is what I've said bad news, and I don't know it?

MEDEA:
You've said what you have said. I don't blame you.

TUTOR:
So—why are you crying? Why are your eyes cast down?

MEDEA:
Old man, I am compelled. The gods and I[46]
1035   devised this strategy. What was I thinking?

---

46. Medea here begins to speak of herself as doing the work of the gods.
The ending of the drama suggests that the gods are in agreement.

TUTOR:
Don't worry now. Your children will bring you home.

MEDEA:
I'll send others home before that day.

TUTOR:
You're not the only woman who's lost her children.
We're mortals. We must bear disasters lightly.

MEDEA:
I'll do as you ask. Now, go inside the house   1040
and see to the children's needs, as usual.

(Exit Tutor into the house.)

Oh, children, children, you two have a city
and home, in which you'll live forever parted
from your mother. You'll leave poor me behind.
I'll travel to another land, an exile,   1045
before I ever have the joy of seeing
you blessed with fortune—before your wedding days,
before I prepare your beds and hold the torches.[47]
My willfulness has cost me all this grief.
I raised you, children, but it was no use;   1050
no use, the way I toiled, how much it hurt,
the pain of childbirth, piercing like a thorn.
And I had so much hope when you were born:
you'd tend to my old age, and when I died,
you'd wrap me in my shroud with your own hands: 1055
an admirable fate for anyone.
That sweet thought has now been crushed. I'll be parted
from both of you, and I will spend my years
in sorrow and in pain. Your eyes no longer
will look upon your mother. You'll move on   1060
to a different life.
                    Oh god, your eyes, the way

---

47. The main event of the Greek wedding ceremony was a nocturnal procession from the house of the bride's family to the groom's. The groom's mother would greet them bearing a torch.

you look at me. Why do you smile, my children,
your very last smile? Aah, what will I do?
The heart goes out of me, women, when I look
1065   at my children's shining eyes. I couldn't do this.
Farewell to the plans I had before.
I'll take my children with me when I leave.
Why should I, just to cause their father pain,
feel twice the pain myself by harming them?
1070   I will not do it. Farewell to my plans.
But wait—what's wrong with me? What do I want?
To allow my enemies to laugh at me?
To let them go unpunished?
                                What I need
is the nerve to do it. I was such a weakling,
1075   to let a soothing word enter my mind.
Children, go inside the house.

> (The children start to go toward the house, but, as
> Medea continues to speak, they continue to watch
> and listen to her, delaying their entry inside.)

                                Whoever
is not permitted to attend these rites,
my sacrifice, let that be his concern.
I won't hold back the force that's in my hand.

Aah!
1080   Oh no, my spirit, please, not that! Don't do it.
Spare the children. Leave them alone, poor thing.
They'll live with me there. They will bring you joy.

By the avenging ones[48] who live below
in Hades, no, I will not leave my children[49]
1085   at the mercy of my enemies' outrage.[xii]
Anyway, the thing's already done.
She won't escape. The crown is on her head.

---

48. The Furies, the primordial spirits of vengeance. See the note at line
1289 below.

49. Medea assumes here that Creon's family will kill her children as
would be required by the laws of vengeance. Jason's first words at his final
arrival indicate that she is correct here.

The royal bride's destroyed, wrapped in her robes.
I know it. Now, since I am setting foot
on a path that will break my heart, and sending them   1090
on one more heartbreaking still, I want to speak
to my children.

    *(Medea reaches toward her children; they come
    back to her.)*

            Children, give me your right hands,
give them to your mother, let me kiss them.
Oh, how I love these hands, how I love these mouths,
the way the children stand, their noble faces!   1095
May fortune bless you—in the other place.
Your father's taken all that once was here.
Oh, your sweet embrace, your tender skin,
your lovely breath, oh children.
                Go now—go.

    (The children go inside.)

I cannot look at them. Grief overwhelms me.   1100
I know that I am working up my nerve[xiii]
for overwhelming evil, yet my spirit
is stronger than my mind's deliberations:
this is the source of mortals' deepest grief.

CHORUS:
    Quite often I've found myself venturing deeper   1105
    than women do normally into discussions
    and subtle distinctions, and I would suggest
    that we have our own Muse, who schools us in wisdom—
    not every woman, but there are a few,
    you'll find one among many, a woman who doesn't   1110
    stand entirely apart from the Muses.

    Here's my opinion: the childless among us,
    the ones who have never experienced parenthood,
    have greater good fortune than those who have children.
    They don't know—how could they?—if children are pleasant   1115
    or hard and distressing. Their lack of experience
    saves them from heartache.

But those who have children, a household's sweet offshoot—
I see them consumed their whole lives with concern.
1120   They fret from the start: are they raising them well?
And then: will they manage to leave them enough?
Then finally: all of this toil and heartache,
is it for children who'll turn out to be
worthless or decent? That much is unclear.

1125   There's one final grief that I'll mention. Supposing
your children have grown up with plenty to live on,
they're healthy, they're decent—if fortune decrees it,
Death comes and spirits their bodies away
down to the Underworld. What is the point, then,
1130   if the gods, adding on to the pains that we mortals
endure for the sake of our children, send death,
most distressing of all? Tell me, where does that leave us?

MEDEA:
My friends, I have been waiting for some time,
keeping watch to see where this will lead.
1135   Look now: here comes one of Jason's men
breathing hard—he seems to be about
to tell us of some new and dreadful act.

(Enter the Messenger from the right.)[50]

MESSENGER:
Medea, run away! Take any ship[xiv]
or wagon that will carry you. Leave now!

MEDEA:
1140   Why should I flee? What makes it necessary?

MESSENGER:
The royal princess and her father Creon
have just now died—the victims of your poison.

---

50. The speech by a messenger late in a drama was a convention in Greek
tragedy. Such narratives allowed the dramatist to depict spectacular deaths
that could not be staged and to include alternative spaces that could not be
accommodated within the Greek theater.

MEDEA:
This news is excellent. From this day forth
I'll count you as a friend and benefactor.

MESSENGER:
What are you saying? Are you sane at all,   1145
or raving? You've attacked the royal hearth—
how can you rejoice, and not be frightened?

MEDEA:
I could tell my own side to this story.
But calm down, friend, and please describe to me
how they were destroyed. If you can say   1150
that they died horribly, I'll feel twice the pleasure.

MESSENGER:
When we saw that your two boys had come
together with their father to the bride's house,
all of us—we servants who have felt
the pain of your misfortunes—were delighted;   1155
the talk was that you'd settled your differences,
you and your husband. We embraced the boys,
kissing their hands, their golden hair. And I,
overjoyed as I was, accompanied
the children to the women's quarters. She—   1160
the mistress we now honor in your place—
before she caught sight of your pair of boys
was gazing eagerly at Jason. Then
she saw the children, and she covered up
her eyes, as if the sight disgusted her,[51]   1165
and turned her pale cheek aside. Your husband
tried to cool down the girl's bad temper,
saying, "Don't be hateful toward your loved ones!
Please, calm your spirit, turn your head this way,
and love those whom your husband loves. Receive   1170
these gifts, and ask your father, for my sake,
not to send these children into exile."
Well, when she saw the fine things, she gave in

---

51. Medea's earlier fears about the welfare of her children under a stepmother are confirmed by the new wife's behavior.

          to everything the man said. They had barely
1175   set foot outside the door—your children and
          their father—when she took the intricate
          embroidered robe and wrapped it round her body,
          and set the golden crown upon her curls,
          and smiled at her bright image—her lifeless double—
1180   in a mirror, as she arranged her hair.
          She rose, and with a delicate step her lovely
          white feet traversed the quarters. She rejoiced
          beyond all measure in the gifts. Quite often
          she extended her ankle, admiring the effect.

1185   What happened next was terrible to see.
          Her skin changed color, and her legs were shaking;
          she reeled sideways, and she would have fallen
          straight to the ground if she hadn't collapsed in her chair.
          Then one of her servants, an old woman,
1190   thinking that the girl must be possessed
          by Pan[52] or by some other god, cried out—
          a shriek of awe and reverence—but when
          she saw the white foam at her mouth, her eyes
          popping out, the blood drained from her face,
1195   she changed her cry to one of bitter mourning.
          A maid ran off to get the princess' father;
          another went to tell the bride's new husband
          of her disaster. Everywhere the sound
          of running footsteps echoed through the house.
1200   And then, in less time than it takes a sprinter
          to cover one leg of a stadium race,
          the girl, whose eyes had been shut tight, awoke,
          poor thing, and she let out a terrible groan,
          for she was being assaulted on two fronts:
1205   the golden garland resting on her head
          sent forth a marvelous stream of all-consuming
          fire, and the delicate robe, the gift
          your children brought, was starting to corrode

---

52. Pan, half man and half goat, was primarily a pastoral god but also
had associations with violent divine possession and was believed to inter-
vene in battles, causing a terror in enemies that acquired the name
"panic." See also *Hippolytus* 142 (158 AS).

the white flesh of that most unfortunate girl.
She jumped up, with flames all over her, 1210
shaking her hair, tossing her head around,
trying to throw the crown off. But the gold
gripped tight, and every movement of her hair
caused the fire to blaze out twice as much.
Defeated by disaster, she fell down 1215
onto the ground, unrecognizable
to anyone but a father. She had lost
the look her eyes had once had, and her face
had lost its beauty. Blood was dripping down,
mixed with fire, from the top of her head 1220
and from her bones the flesh was peeling back
like resin, shorn by unseen jaws of poison,
terrible to see. We all were frightened
to touch the corpse. We'd seen what had just happened.
But her poor father took us by surprise: 1225
he ran into the room and threw himself—
not knowing any better—on her corpse.
He moaned, and wrapped her in his arms, and kissed her,
crying, "Oh, my poor unhappy child,
what god dishonors you? What god destroys you? 1230
Who has taken you away from me,
an old man who has one foot in the grave?
Let me die with you, child." When he was done
with his lament, he tried to straighten up
his agèd body, but the delicate robe 1235
clung to him as ivy clings to laurel,
and then a terrible wrestling match began.
He tried to flex his knee; she pulled him back.
If he used force, he tore the agèd flesh
off of his bones. He finally gave up, 1240
unlucky man; his soul slipped away
when he could fight no longer. There they lie,
two corpses, a daughter and her aged father,
side by side, a disaster that longs for tears.

About your situation, I am silent. 1245
You realize what penalty awaits you.
About our mortal lives, I feel the way
I've often felt before: we are mere shadows.

I wouldn't hesitate to say that those
1250   who seem so wise, who deal in subtleties—
they earn the prize for being the greatest fools.
For really, there is no man blessed with fortune.
One man might be luckier, more prosperous
than someone else, but no man's ever blessed.

(Exit the Messenger to the right.)

CHORUS:
1255   On this day fortune has bestowed on Jason
much grief, it seems, as justice has demanded.
Poor thing, we pity you for this disaster,
daughter of Creon, you who have descended
to Hades' halls because of your marriage to Jason.

MEDEA:
1260   My friends, it is decided: as soon as possible
I must kill my children and leave this land
before I give my enemies a chance
to slaughter them with a hand that's moved by hatred.
They must die anyway, and since they must,
1265   I will kill them. I'm the one who bore them.
Arm yourself, my heart. Why am I waiting
to do this terrible, necessary crime?
Unhappy hand, act now. Take up the sword,
just take it; approach the starting post of pain
1270   to last a lifetime; do not weaken, don't
remember that you love your children dearly,
that you gave them life. For one short day
forget your children. Afterward, you'll grieve.
For even if you kill them, they were yours;
1275   you loved them. I'm a woman cursed by fortune.

(Medea enters the house.)[53]

---

53. Medea has been onstage since her first entrance; she has remained
through all of the negotiations, meetings, supplications, and choral odes.
She finally leaves to commit the horrific murders of her children, and the
impact of her departure is intensified by its long delay.

CHORUS:

[Strophe 1]

O Earth, O radiant beam
of Helios, look down and see her—
this woman, destroyer, before she can lay
her hand stained with blood,
her kin-killing hand   1280
upon her own children
descended from you
the gods' golden race;
for such blood to spill
at the hands of a mortal   1285
fills us with fear.
Light born from Zeus,
stop her, remove
this bloodstained Erinys;[54]
take her away   1290
from this house cursed with vengeance.

[Antistrophe 1]

Your toil has all been in vain,
in vain, all the heartache of raising
your children, your dearest, O sorrowful one
who once left behind   1295
the dark Clashing Rocks
most hostile to strangers.
What burden of rage
descended upon
your mind? Why does wild   1300
slaughter follow on slaughter?
Blood-spatter, stain,
slaughter of kin,
murder within
the family brings grief   1305

---

54. Erinys was a Fury, one of the primordial beings born from the castration of the first king of the gods, Ouranos (Sky). The Furies were believed to punish those who spill kindred blood; hence, in Aeschylus' *Oresteia*, they pursue Orestes after he kills his mother, Clytemnestra.

tuned to the crime
from the gods to the household.

CHILD:

(From within the house.)[55]

Oh no!

CHORUS:

[Strophe 2]

Do you hear the shouts, the shouts of her children?
Poor woman: she's cursed, undone by her fortune.

CHILD 1:

1310   Oh, how can I escape my mother's hand?

CHILD 2:

Dear brother, I don't know. We are destroyed.

CHORUS:

Shall I go inside?
I ought to prevent this,
the slaughter of children.

CHILD 1:

1315   Yes, come and stop her! That is what we need.

CHILD 2:

We're trapped; we're caught! The sword is at our throats.

CHORUS:

Poor thing: after all
you were rock, you were iron:
to reap with your own hand
1320   the crop that you bore;
to cut down your kin
with a fate-dealing hand.

---

55. Both of the actors are offstage and thus their voices are available to
take the parts of the boys.

[Antistrophe 2]

I've heard of just one, just one other woman
who dared to attack, to hurt her own children:

Ino, whom the gods once drove insane   1325
and Zeus's wife sent wandering from her home.[56]

The poor woman leapt
to sea with her children:
an unholy slaughter.

She stepped down from a steep crag's rocky edge   1330
and died with her two children in the waves.

What terrible deed
could surpass such an outrage?
O bed of their marriage,
O woman's desire: 1335
such harm have you done,
so much pain have you caused.

(Enter Jason from the right.)

JASON:
Women, you who stand here near the house—
is she at home, Medea, the perpetrator
of all these terrors, or has she gone away?   1340
Oh yes, she'll have to hide beneath the earth
or lift her body into the sky with wings
to escape the royal family's cry for justice.
Does she think she can murder this land's rulers

---

56. Ino was one of the daughters of Cadmus who participated in the dis-
memberment of Pentheus while under the spell of Dionysus. She then
became the second wife of King Athamas of Iolcus and almost had his
sons by his first wife killed (the "evil stepmother" motif again). Hera
drove Ino and Athamas mad so that Athamas killed one of the sons Ino
had borne to him and Ino leapt into the sea with the other. The Chorus
here elide other myths of Greek mothers who kill their children, including
Agavê (Ino's sister and Pentheus' mother), Althaea (the mother of the
Calydonian hero Meleager), and Procne (see the note at line 232 above).
Perhaps this elision is meant to stress the supreme horror of the deed by
imagining that only one other could perform it.

1345   then simply flee this house, with no requital?
           I'm worried about the children more than her—
           the ones she's hurt will pay her back in kind.
           I've come to save my children, save their lives.
           The family might retaliate, might strike
1350   the children for their mother's unholy slaughter.

CHORUS:
           Poor man. Jason, if you realized
           how bad it was, you wouldn't have said that.

JASON:
           What is it? Does she want to kill *me* now?

CHORUS:
           Your children are dead, killed by their mother's hand.

JASON:
1355   What are you saying, women? You have destroyed me.

CHORUS:
           Please understand: your children no longer exist.

JASON:
           Where did she kill them? Inside the house, or outside?

CHORUS:
           Open the gates; you'll see your children's slaughter.

JASON:
           Servants, quick, open the door, unbar it;
1360   undo the bolts, and let me see this double
           evil: their dead bodies, and the one
           whom I will bring to justice.

                   (*Medea appears above the roof in a flying chariot,
                   with the bodies of the children.*)⁵⁷

---

57. As if the scenario were not shocking enough, Medea appears on the
mêchanê, a platform suspended by a crane that was used in the Greek theater typically, if not exclusively, for appearances by gods at a drama's end,

MEDEA:

                Why are you trying
to pry those gates? Is it their corpses you seek,
and me, the perpetrator? Stop your struggle.
If you need something, ask me. Speak your mind.   1365
But you will never touch us with your hand.
My father's father, Helios, gives me safety
from hostile hands. This chariot protects me.

JASON:
  You hateful thing, O woman most detested
  by the gods, by me, by all mankind—   1370
  you dared to strike your children with a sword,
  children you bore yourself. You have destroyed me,
  left me childless. And yet you live, you look
  upon the sun and earth, you who had the nerve
  to do this most unholy deed. I wish   1375
  you would die. I have more sense now than I had
  the day I took you from your barbarian land
  and brought you to a Greek home—you're a plague,
  betrayer of your father and the land
  that raised you. But the gods have sent the vengeance   1380
  that *you* deserve to crash down on *my* head.
  You killed your brother right at home, then climbed
  aboard the *Argo* with its lovely prow.
  That's how your career began. You married
  me, and bore me children. For the sake   1385
  of passion, of your bed, you have destroyed them.
  No Greek woman[58] would have had the nerve
  to do this, but I married you instead:

---

usually to solve crises, tie up loose ends, or denounce humans; we use the
Latin translation of this phenomenon, deus ex machina, to designate such
interventions. Euripides was criticized by Aristotle for his reliance on this
device, which he also deploys in, among other plays, *Electra, Ion, Iphigenia among the Taurians,* and the *Bacchae.* Medea's violent denunciation of
Jason anticipates the similar language of Dionysus toward the Theban
royal family at the end of the *Bacchae.*

58. As the Chorus have mentioned (1323–31), there is at least one earlier
story of a Greek woman guilty of filicide—and Euripides' audience would
have known of others.

a hateful bond. You ruined me. You're not
1390   a woman; you're a lion, with a nature
more wild than Scylla's, the Etruscan freak.⁵⁹
I couldn't wound you with ten thousand insults;
there's nothing you can't take. Get out of here,
you filth, you child-murderer. For me,
1395   all that's left is tears for my misfortune.
I'll never have the joy of my bride's bed,
nor will I ever again speak to my children,
my children, whom I raised. And now I've lost them.ˣᵛ

MEDEA:
I would have made a long speech in reply
1400   to yours, if father Zeus were unaware
of what I've done for you, and how you've acted.
You dishonored my bed. There was no way
you could go on to lead a pleasant life,
to laugh at me—not you, and not the princess;
1405   nor could Creon, who arranged your marriage,
exile me and walk away unpunished.
So go ahead, call me a lion, call me
a Scylla, skulking in her Etruscan cave.
I've done what I had to do. I've jabbed your heart.

JASON:
1410   You feel the pain yourself. This hurts you, too.

MEDEA:
The pain is good, as long as you're not laughing.

JASON:
O children, you were cursed with an evil mother.

---

59. Scylla was a monstrous female giant with twelve feet and six heads,
and various canine elements, as described in Books 11 and 12 of Homer's
Odyssey. She lived opposite the whirlpool Charybdis, and sailors had to
choose toward which of the two they would navigate. In the art of the
fifth century BCE, Scylla was depicted as an attractive woman above,
with a row of dog heads around her waist and a fish tail below. Jason
calls her "Etruscan" (in the Greek, "Tyrsenian"), locating her in the Tyr-
rhenian Sea.

MEDEA:
O sons, you were destroyed by your father's sickness.

JASON:
My right hand is not the one that killed them.

MEDEA:
Your outrage, and your newfound bride, destroyed them.   1415

JASON:
The bedroom was enough to make you kill?

MEDEA:
Does that pain mean so little to a woman?

JASON:
Yes,
to one with wise restraint. To you, it's everything.

MEDEA:
They exist no longer. That will sting you.

JASON:
They exist. They live to avenge your crime.   1420

MEDEA:
The gods know who was first to cause this pain.

JASON:
Oh yes. They know your mind. They spit on it.

MEDEA:
Go on and hate me. I detest your voice.

JASON:
I feel the same. That makes it easy to leave you.

MEDEA:
What shall I do, then? I'd like nothing better.   1425

JASON:
Let me bury their bodies. Let me grieve.

MEDEA:
   Forget it. I will take them away myself
   and bury them with this hand, in the precinct
   sacred to Hera of the rocky heights.
1430   No enemy will treat their graves with outrage.
   To this land of Sisyphus[60] I bequeath
   a holy festival, a ritual
   to expiate in times to come this most
   unholy slaughter.[61] I myself will go
1435   to live together with Pandion's son
   Aegeus, in Erechtheus's city.
   And you, an evil man, as you deserve,
   will die an evil death, struck on the head
   by a fragment of the *Argo*.[62] You will see
1440   how bitter was the outcome of my marriage.

   *(Here the meter changes from spoken dialogue to
   chanted anapests.)*[63]

JASON:
   May you be destroyed by the children's Erinys
   and bloodthirsty Justice!

MEDEA:
                  What spirit, what god
   listens to you, you liar, you breaker
   of oaths, you deceiver of guests?

---

60. Corinth was the home of Sisyphus, the notorious deceiver; see the note at line 414 above.

61. One of Hera's cult titles in Corinth was *Akraia*, "of the rocky heights," and there was a sanctuary to her by that name there. Pausanias 2.3.6 confirms that there was a sacred festival such as Medea describes here. A number of Euripidean tragedies end with the establishment of a cult; compare *Hippolytus* 1423–30 (1591–1601 AS).

62. Jason will meet an utterly unheroic end, since the hero's goal is a glorious death in battle, not from a rotten piece of a ship.

63. The anapestic meter was often used for exits and thus signals closure. Here the meter also recalls the chanted laments, in anapests, of Medea in the first scene.

JASON:
                                    You are loathsome.
You murdered your children.

MEDEA:
                                    Get out of here, go—
go bury your wife.   1445

JASON:
                        I'm leaving, bereft
of my sons.

MEDEA:
            Do you think that you're mourning them now?
Just wait till you're old.

JASON:
Oh, dearest children.

MEDEA:
                                    To me, not to you.

JASON:
And yet you still did this?

MEDEA:

                                    To make you feel pain.   1450

JASON:
I wish I could hold them and kiss them, my children.

MEDEA:
You long for them now and you want to embrace them,
but you are the one who pushed them away.

JASON:
By the gods, let me touch the soft skin of my children.

MEDEA:
No. What's the point? You are wasting your words.   1455

*(The chariot flies away with Medea and the bodies
of the children.)*

JASON:
  Zeus, do you hear how I'm driven away,
  do you see what I suffer at her loathsome hands,
  this lion, this child-killer!
                              With all my strength
  I mourn for them now and I call on the gods
1460   and spirits to witness that you killed my children
  and now won't allow me to touch them or bury them.
  I wish now that I'd never fathered them,[xvi] only
  to see them extinguished, to see what you've done.

  *(Exit Jason to the right, accompanied by the
  Chorus.)*

CHORUS:
  Zeus on Olympus enforces all things;
1465   the gods can accomplish what no one would hope for.
  What we expect may not happen at all,
  while the gods find a way, against all expectation,
  to do what they want, however surprising.
  And that is exactly how this case turned out.[xvii]

Endnotes and Comments on the Text

In the notes below I have translated, for the sake of completeness, lines that appear in the manuscripts of Euripides but are not considered genuine by modern editors, who mark such lines as probable interpolations by putting them in square brackets. Additions to the text after Euripides' lifetime may have been made by actors (Euripides' plays were performed often in the centuries following his death) or by scribes copying the texts; the earliest manuscripts we have of Euripides' plays are from the Middle Ages and reflect many stages of copying and recopying. An actor might insert a line or passage from another play to please the audience; similarly, a scribe might copy a "parallel passage" into the margin of his text, which a later copyist might insert into the text itself. On the history of the texts, see Page (1971), pp. xxxvii–lvii and Csapo and Slater (1995), pp. 1–38.

I have also noted lines that I have kept in the text in spite of editors' objections (it seems to me not impossible that Euripides himself would repeat a line or phrase), and pointed out some patterns of language in the Greek (see notes ix, xv, and xvi).

—DAS

i. I have omitted the following line (41 in the Greek text): "creeping silently into their bedroom." See Willink (1988) for the deletion of this line and a defense of the surrounding lines. Compare line 387 (379 in the Greek) and note vii below.

ii. The following line (87 in the Greek text) was condemned by ancient commentators, and modern editors continue to reject it as intrusive:

Some with good reason, some for the sake of gain.

iii. I retain this line, 246 in the Greek (reading Porson's *hêlikas* to solve the metrical problem), though most editors, following Wilamowitz, reject it as an interpolation. See Podlecki (1989) and Mastronarde (2002), *ad loc.*

iv. I omit the following line, 262 in the Greek:

the daughter whom he married, and her father.

Most editors follow Lenting (1820) in deleting this as an interpolation based on line 288 (295 AS). The Greek is unidiomatic, and the line is distracting and ineffective.

v. I retain this line (304 in the Greek), although it was deleted by Pierson (1752) and is still considered an interpolation by most editors, in part because of its similarity to line 808 of the Greek (830 AS).

vi. See Kovacs (1987), pp. 267–68, on the text of lines 357–61 of the Greek (366–69 AS).

vii. I omit the following line (379 Greek):

or thrust a sharpened knife-blade through the liver

See Willink (1988), and compare line 47 of the translation (40 of the Greek text), and note i above.

viii. The same line (468 of the Greek text) is found at 1324 (1369–70 AS), where Jason flings it back at Medea after calling her "most detested." Most editors (following Brunck 1779) delete the line here; see Mastronarde's (2002) commentary on 468. In my view, the line is appropriate in both contexts.

ix. With the phrase "saved your life" (cf. 481 above), Medea brings her argument to a close. This technique of beginning and ending with the same words (ring composition) is used on a smaller scale in Jason's speech above, with the words "You are now an exile" (453, 464).

x. The following line ("to the bride, to be exempt from exile," 785 in the Greek), omitted here, is grammatically awkward. It is not present in all manuscripts, and most editors (since Valckenaer) have rejected it.

xi. I omit the following two lines, 1006–7 in the Greek text:

Why have you turned your face away? Why aren't you
happy to hear what I have had to say?

They are repeated almost exactly from 923–24 (946–49 AS). See Mastronarde (2002, *ad loc.*).

xii. Lines 1062–63 omitted:

They must die anyway, and since they must,
I will kill them. I'm the one who bore them.

These lines are also found in the manuscripts at 1240–41 (1264–65 AS), where they fit the context better.

xiii. Reading *tolmêsô*, with the majority of the manuscripts, in line 1078 of the Greek.

xiv. The preceding line ("You who have done this terrible lawless deed," 1121 of the Greek text), omitted here, is missing from some of the manuscripts, and many editors have deleted it, following Lenting (1820).

xv. Euripides here uses a verb that means both "destroyed" and "lost," and that punctuates the sections of Jason's speech; it occurs at the end of line 1326 of the Greek (*apôlesas*, "you have destroyed"; 1372 AS), and twelve lines later at 1338 (*apôlesas* again; 1386 AS); his speech ends another twelve lines later with *apôlesa*, "I've lost" (1350; 1398 AS). The effect of this patterned repetition and the double meaning of *apôlesa* ("I have destroyed") is striking. Jason uses the verb again at 1365 (1414 AS).

This verb is frequent in Euripides, and Aristophanes may have been making fun of (among other things) the tragedian's fondness for it in the *lêkythion apôlesen* scene of *Frogs* (1208 ff). The character Aeschylus ridicules the character Euripides by completing several of his verses with this phrase, which means "lost his little oil jar."

xvi. The play ends as it began, with a character wishing that all this had never happened: the Nurse, line 1, *Eith' ôphel' ... mê ...*; here, *mêpot' ... ophelon*, 1413 (1462 AS).

xvii. These last six lines (in chanted anapests) are also found at the end of four other plays by Euripides: *Alcestis, Andromache, Helen,* and the *Bacchae*. In all of the other plays, the first line of the coda is "The designs of the deities take many forms"; here (1464) "Zeus the enforcer" is recognized (cf. 171). We do not know whether Euripides himself ended each of these plays with this coda, or if it was added by actors or editors. For the latter view, see Mastronarde (2002) on *Medea* 1415–19. For the former, in the case of *Medea*, and a defense of the significance of Zeus in the variation, see Kovacs (1987, pp. 268–70, and 1993). On codas in Sophocles and Euripides, see Roberts (1987).

Select Bibliography

This (very selective) list focuses on relatively recent scholarship written in English, which is for the most part available in good university libraries. When important articles have been republished in prominent collections of essays, only the new publication information is cited.

Editions, Commentaries, and Textual Discussions

Allen, James T., and Gabriel Italie, eds. *A Concordance to Euripides.* Berkeley and London: University of California Press and Cambridge University Press, 1954.

Diggle, J., ed. *Euripidis Fabulae.* Vol. 1. New York: Oxford University Press, 1984.

Kovacs, David. "Treading the Circle Warily: Literary Criticism and the Text of Euripides." *Transactions of the American Philological Association* 117 (1987): 257–70.

———, ed. and trans. *Euripides I:* Cyclops, Alcestis, Medea. Cambridge, MA: Harvard University Press, 1994. Repr. with corrections 2001.

Mastronarde, Donald J., ed. and comm. *Euripides:* Medea. New York: Cambridge University Press, 2002.

Page, Denys L. *Euripides:* Medea. Oxford: Clarendon Press, 1938. Repr. with corrections 1971.

Podlecki, Anthony J., trans. and comm. *Euripides'* Medea. Newburyport, MA: Focus Classical Library, 1989.

Roberts, Deborah H. "Parting Words: Final Lines in Sophocles and Euripides." *Classical Quarterly* 37 (1987): 51–64.

Willink, C. W. "Eur. *Medea* 1–45, 371–85." *Classical Quarterly* 38 (1988): 313–23.

Works on Greek Theater and Society

Arrowsmith, William. "A Greek Theater of Ideas." In Erich Segal, ed. (1968), pp. 13–33.

Belfiore, Elizabeth S. *Murder among Friends: Violation of* Philia *in Greek Tragedy.* New York: Oxford University Press, 2000.

Buxton, R. G. A. *Persuasion in Greek Tragedy: A Study of* Peitho. New York: Cambridge University Press, 1982.

Cairns, Douglas L. Aidôs: *The Psychology and Ethics of Honour and Shame in Ancient Greek Literature.* Oxford: Oxford University Press, 1993.

Csapo, Eric, and William J. Slater. *The Context of Ancient Drama.* Ann Arbor: University of Michigan Press, 1995.

Easterling, P. E., ed. *The Cambridge Companion to Greek Tragedy.* Cambridge: Cambridge University Press, 1997.

Easterling, P. E., and Bernard Knox, eds. *The Cambridge History of Classical Literature.* Vol. 1, *Greek Literature.* Cambridge: Cambridge University Press, 1985.

Foley, Helene P. "Modern Performance and Adaptation of Greek Tragedy." *Transactions of the American Philological Association* 129 (1999): 1–12.

——. *Female Acts in Greek Tragedy.* Princeton, NJ: Princeton University Press, 2001.

Golder, Herbert, and Stephen Scully, eds. "The Chorus in Greek Tragedy and Culture." *Arion* 3.1 and 4.1 (1994–96).

Goldhill, Simon. *Reading Greek Tragedy.* Cambridge: Cambridge University Press, 1986.

——. "The Great Dionysia and Civic Ideology." In John J. Winkler and Froma I. Zeitlin, eds. (1990), pp. 97–129.

Goldhill, Simon, and Robin Osborne, eds. *Performance Culture and Athenian Democracy.* Cambridge: Cambridge University Press, 1999.

Gregory, Justina, ed. *A Companion to Greek Tragedy.* Malden, MA: Blackwell, 2005.

Griffin, Jasper. "The Social Function of Attic Tragedy." *Classical Quarterly* 48 (1998): 39–61.

Hall, Edith. *Inventing the Barbarian: Greek Self-Definition through Tragedy.* New York: Oxford University Press, 1989.

Henderson, J. "Women and the Athenian Dramatic Festivals." *Transactions of the American Philological Association* 121 (1991): 133–47.

Jones, John. *On Aristotle and Greek Tragedy.* London: Chatto and Windus, 1962.

Knox, Bernard. *Word and Action: Essays on the Ancient Theater.* Baltimore, MD: Johns Hopkins University Press, 1979.

Lefkowitz, Mary. *The Lives of the Greek Poets.* Baltimore, MD: Johns Hopkins University Press, 1981.

Lesky, Albin. *Greek Tragic Poetry.* Translated by Matthew Dillon. New Haven, CT: Yale University Press, 1983.

McClure, Laura. *Spoken Like a Woman: Speech and Gender in Athenian Drama.* Princeton, NJ: Princeton University Press, 1999.

Mitchell-Boyask, Robin. *Plague and the Athenian Imagination: Drama, History, and the Cult of Asclepius.* Cambridge: Cambridge University Press, 2008.

Nussbaum, Martha. *The Fragility of Goodness: Luck and Ethics in Greek Tragedy and Philosophy.* Cambridge: Cambridge University Press, 1986.

Rehm, Rush. *Greek Tragic Theatre.* New York: Routledge, 1992.

———. *Marriage to Death: The Conflation of Wedding and Funeral Rituals in Greek Tragedy.* Princeton, NJ: Princeton University Press, 1994.

Seaford, Richard. "The Social Function of Attic Tragedy: A Response to Jasper Griffin." *Classical Quarterly* 50 (2000): 30–44.

Segal, Charles. *Interpreting Greek Tragedy: Myth, Poetry, Text.* Ithaca, NY: Cornell University Press, 1986.

Silk, M. S., ed. *Tragedy and the Tragic: Greek Theatre and Beyond.* Oxford: Oxford University Press, 1996.

Strauss, Barry S. *Fathers and Sons in Athens: Ideology and Society in the Era of the Peloponnesian War.* Princeton, NJ: Princeton University Press, 1993.

Taplin, Oliver. *Greek Tragedy in Action.* Berkeley: University of California Press, 1978.

Vernant, Jean-Pierre, and Pierre Vidal-Naquet. *Myth and Tragedy in Ancient Greece.* Translated by Janet Lloyd. New York: Zone Books, 1988.

Wiles, David. *Tragedy in Athens: Performance Space and Theatrical Meaning.* New York: Cambridge University Press, 1997.

Winkler, John J., and Froma I. Zeitlin, eds. *Nothing to Do with Dionysos? Athenian Drama in Its Social Context.* Princeton, NJ: Princeton University Press, 1990.

Wohl, Victoria. *Intimate Commerce: Exchange, Gender, and Subjectivity in Greek Tragedy.* Austin: University of Texas Press, 1998.

Zeitlin, Froma I. *Playing the Other: Gender and Society in Classical Greek Literature.* Chicago: University of Chicago Press, 1996.

General Works on Euripides

Arnott, W. G. "Euripides and the Unexpected." *Greece and Rome* 20 (1984): 49–64.

Barlow, Shirley A. *The Imagery of Euripides: A Study in the Dramatic Use of Pictorial Language.* 2nd ed. Bristol: Bristol Classical Press, 1986.

Burian, Peter, ed. *Directions in Euripidean Criticism*. Durham, NC: Duke University Press, 1985.

Collard, Christopher. *Euripides*. Greece and Rome: New Surveys in the Classics, 14. Oxford: Clarendon Press, 1981.

Conacher, D. J. *Euripidean Drama: Myth, Theme and Structure*. Toronto: University of Toronto Press, 1967.

Dunn, Francis M. *Tragedy's End: Closure and Innovation in Euripidean Drama*. New York: Oxford University Press, 1996.

Fletcher, Judith. "Women and Oaths in Euripides." *Theatre Journal* 55 (2003): 29–44.

Foley, Helene P. *Ritual Irony: Poetry and Sacrifice in Euripides*. Ithaca, NY: Cornell University Press, 1985.

Gregory, Justina. *Euripides and the Instruction of the Athenians*. Ann Arbor: University of Michigan Press, 1991.

———. "Euripides as Social Critic." *Greece and Rome* 49 (2002): 145–62.

Halleran, Michael R. *The Stagecraft in Euripides*. London: Croom Helm, 1985.

Meltzer, Gary S. *Euripides and the Poetics of Nostalgia*. Cambridge: Cambridge University Press, 2006.

Michelini, Ann N. *Euripides and the Tragic Tradition*. Madison: University of Wisconsin Press, 1987.

Mitchell-Boyask, Robin, ed. *Approaches to Teaching the Dramas of Euripides*. New York: Modern Language Association of America, 2002.

Mossman, Judith, ed. *Oxford Readings in Classical Studies: Euripides*. New York: Oxford University Press, 2003.

Powell, Anton, ed. *Euripides, Women, and Sexuality*. London and New York: Routledge, 1990.

Rabinowitz, Nancy Sorkin. *Anxiety Veiled: Euripides and the Traffic in Women*. Ithaca, NY: Cornell University Press, 1993.

Sansone, David. "Plato and Euripides." *Illinois Classical Studies* 21 (1996): 35–61.

Scullion, S. "Euripides and Macedon, or the Silence of the Frogs." *Classical Quarterly* 53 (2003): 389–400.

Segal, Charles. *Euripides and the Poetics of Sorrow: Art, Gender, and Commemoration in* Alcestis, Hippolytus, *and* Hecuba. Durham, NC: Duke University Press, 1993.

Segal, Erich, ed. *Euripides: A Collection of Critical Essays*. Englewood Cliffs, NJ: Prentice-Hall, 1968.

Winnington-Ingram, R. P. "Euripides: *Poietes Sophos*." In Judith Mossman, ed. (2003), pp. 47–63.

Studies of *Medea*

Allan, William. *Euripides:* Medea. Duckworth Companions to Greek and Roman Tragedy. London: Duckworth, 2002.

Barlow, S. A. "Stereotype and Reversal in Euripides' *Medea*." *Greece and Rome* 36 (1989): 158–71.

Boedeker, Deborah. "Euripides' *Medea* and the Vanity of *Logoi*." *Classical Philology* 86 (1991): 95–112.

Burnett, Anne. "Medea and the Tragedy of Revenge." *Classical Philology* 68 (1973): 1–24.

Clauss, James J., and Sarah Iles Johnston, eds. *Medea: Essays on Medea in Myth, Literature, Philosophy, and Art*. Princeton, NJ: Princeton University Press, 1997.

Easterling, P. E. "The Infanticide in Euripides' *Medea*." In Judith Mossman, ed. (2003), pp. 187–200.

Gellrich, Michelle. "Medea Hypokrites." *Arethusa* 35 (2002): 315–37.

Hall, Edith, Fiona Macintosh, and Oliver Taplin, eds. *Medea in Performance, 1500–2000*. Oxford: Legenda, 2000.

Kovacs, David. "Zeus in Euripides' *Medea*." *American Journal of Philology* 114 (1993): 45–70.

McDermott, Emily A. *Euripides' Medea: The Incarnation of Disorder*. University Park: Pennsylvania State University Press, 1989.

Mueller, Melissa. "The Language of Reciprocity in Euripides' *Medea*." *American Journal of Philology* 122 (2001): 471–504.

Sfyroeras, P. "The Ironies of Salvation: The Aigeus Scene in Euripides' *Medea*." *Classical Journal* 90 (1995): 125–42.

(See also chapters in Dunn, Foley 2001, Knox, Mitchell-Boyask 2002, Rabinowitz, and Rehm 1994. For a more detailed bibliography, see Allan.)